How to
Create and Use
RUBRICS

for FORMATIVE ASSESSMENT
and GRADING

ASCD MEMBER BOOK

How to
Create and Use
RUBRICS

for FORMATIVE ASSESSMENT and GRADING

Susan M. Brookhart

ascd

Arlington, Virginia USA

2800 Shirlington Road, Suite 1001 • Arlington, VA 22206 USA
Phone: 800-933-2723 or 703-578-9600 • Fax: 703-575-5400
Website: www.ascd.org • E-mail: member@ascd.org
Author guidelines: www.ascd.org/write

Gene R. Carter, *Executive Director;* Mary Catherine (MC) Desrosiers, *Chief Program Development Officer;* Richard Papale, *Publisher;* Genny Ostertag, *Acquisitions Editor;* Julie Houtz, *Director, Book Editing & Production;* Deborah Siegel, *Editor;* Louise Bova, *Senior Graphic Designer;* Mike Kalyan, *Production Manager;* Keith Demmons, *Desktop Publishing Specialist;* Kyle Steichen, *Production Specialist*

Cover art © 2013 by ASCD. ASCD publications present a variety of viewpoints. The views expressed or implied in this book should not be interpreted as official positions of the Association.

All web links in this book are correct as of the publication date below but may have become inactive or otherwise modified since that time. If you notice a deactivated or changed link, please e-mail books@ascd.org with the words "Link Update" in the subject line. In your message, please specify the web link, the book title, and the page number on which the link appears.

ASCD Member Book, No. FY13-4 (Jan. 2013, PSI+). ASCD Member Books mail to Premium (P), Select (S), and Institutional Plus (I+) members on this schedule: Jan., PSI+; Feb., P; Apr., PSI+; May, P; July, PSI+; Aug., P; Sept., PSI+; Nov., PSI+; Dec., P. Select membership was formerly known as Comprehensive membership.

PAPERBACK ISBN: 978-1-4166-1507-1 ASCD product #112001
Also available as an e-book (see Books in Print for the ISBNs).
Quantity discounts: 10–49 copies, 10%; 50+ copies, 15%; for 1,000 or more copies, call 800-933-2723, ext. 5773, or 703-575-5773. For desk copies: www.ascd.org/deskcopy

Library of Congress Cataloging-in-Publication Data
Brookhart, Susan M.
How to create and use rubrics for formative assessment and grading / Susan M. Brookhart.
    p. cm.
 Includes bibliographical references and index.
 ISBN 978-1-4166-1507-1 (pbk. : alk. paper)
1. Grading and marking (Students) 2. Educational evaluation. I. Title.
LB3051.B7285 2013
371.26–dc23
                        2012037286

30 29 28 27 26 25 24 24 23 22   8 9 10 11 12

To my daughter Rachel Brookhart,
with love and thanks for all her help and support.

How to
Create and Use
RUBRICS for FORMATIVE ASSESSMENT and GRADING

Preface

The purpose of this book, as the title suggests, is to help you use rubrics in the classroom. To do that, two criteria must be met. First, the rubrics themselves must be well designed. Second, the rubrics should be used for learning as well as for grading.

Many of you are already familiar with rubrics, and you will read this book through the lens of what you already know. For some, the book will be an affirmation of your current understanding of rubrics and provide (I hope) some additional suggestions and examples. But for others, the book may challenge your currently held views and practices regarding rubrics and call for some change.

So I wrote this book with some apprehension. It's always a challenge to "come in in the middle" of something. Teachers do that all the time, however. I ask all of you to keep an open mind and to constantly ask yourself, "What do I think about this?" To that end, I have included self-reflection questions along the way. I encourage you to think about them, perhaps keeping a journal of these reflections so you can review and consolidate your own learning at the end.

In some ways, this book is two books in one, and for that reason it is divided into Part I and Part II. Part I is about rubrics themselves: what they are, how to write them, and some examples of different kinds of rubrics. Part II is about how to use rubrics in your teaching.

The big ideas in Part I concern the two must-have aspects of rubrics. First, rubrics must have clear and appropriate criteria about the learning students will be demonstrating (not about the task). Second, rubrics must have clear descriptions of performance over a continuum of quality. If the rubrics are analytic, each criterion will have separate descriptions of performance. If the rubrics are holistic, the descriptions of performance for each level will consider all the criteria simultaneously.

The big idea in Part II is that rubrics should assist with learning as well as assess it. The strategies in Part II are grouped according to purpose: sharing learning targets with students, formative assessment in terms of feedback and student self-evaluation, and grading. Actually, sharing learning targets with students is the foundational formative assessment strategy. Without clear learning targets, from the students' point of view there is nothing to assess.

Acknowledgments

I am grateful for the support, help, and assistance of many people. Thanks to the amazing Bev Long and the educators in Armstrong School District, to the incredible Connie Moss and the Center for Advancing the Study of Teaching and Learning in the School of Education at Duquesne University, to wonderful colleagues Judy Arter and Jan Chappuis, and to all the dedicated educators over the years with whom I've been fortunate to have conversations about rubrics and about student learning. I have learned from you all. Thanks to the talented editorial and production staff at ASCD, especially Genny Ostertag and Deborah Siegel. Thanks to my family, especially my husband Frank for his love and support, to my daughter Rachel for help especially with the Rubric for Laughing, and to my daughter Carol for hanging in there. This work has been inspired by all of you. Of course, any errors or omissions are mine alone.

Part I

All Kinds of
RUBRICS

1

What Are Rubrics and Why Are They Important?

The word *rubric* comes from the Latin word for *red*. The online Merriam-Webster dictionary lists the first meaning of *rubric* as "an authoritative rule" and the fourth meaning as "a guide listing specific criteria for grading or scoring academic papers, projects, or tests." How did the name for a color come to mean a rule or guide? At least as far back as the Middle Ages, the rules for the conduct of liturgical services—as opposed to the actual spoken words of the liturgy—were often printed in red, so the rules were "the red things" on the page.

In this book, I will show that rubrics for classroom use are both *more* and *less* than the dictionary definition suggests. They are more because rubrics are good for much more than just grading or scoring. They are less because not just any set of rules or guides for student work are rubrics. This first chapter lays out some basic concepts about rubrics. Chapter 2 illustrates common misconceptions about rubrics, and Chapter 3 describes how to write or select effective rubrics.

SELF-REFLECTION

What is your current view of rubrics? Write down what you know about them and what experiences you have had using them. Save this reflection to compare with a similar reflection after you have read this book.

What is a rubric?

A rubric is a coherent set of criteria for students' work that includes descriptions of levels of performance quality on the criteria. Sounds simple enough, right? Unfortunately, this definition of *rubric* is rarely demonstrated in practice. The Internet, for example, offers many rubrics that do not, in fact, describe performance. I think I know why that might be and will explain that in Chapter 2, but for now let's start with the positive. It should be clear from the definition that rubrics have two major aspects: *coherent sets of criteria* and *descriptions of levels of performance* for these criteria.

The genius of rubrics is that they are descriptive and not evaluative. Of course, rubrics can be used to evaluate, but the operating principle is you match the performance to the description rather than "judge" it. Thus rubrics are as good or bad as the criteria selected and the descriptions of the levels of performance under each. Effective rubrics have appropriate criteria and well-written descriptions of performance.

What is the purpose of rubrics?

Like any other evaluation tool, rubrics are useful for certain purposes and not for others. *The main purpose of rubrics is to assess performances.* For some performances, you observe the student in the process of doing something, like using an electric drill or discussing an issue. For other performances, you observe the product that is the result of the student's work, like a finished bookshelf or a written report. Figure 1.1 lists some common kinds of school performances that can be assessed with rubrics. This list by no means covers every possible school performance. It is just meant to help you think of the types of performances you might assess with rubrics.

This list is not meant to suggest what your students *should* perform. State standards, curriculum goals, and instructional goals and objectives are the sources for what types of performances your students should be able to do. When the intended learning outcomes are best indicated by performances—things students would do, make, say, or write—then rubrics are the best way to assess them. Notice that the performances themselves are not learning outcomes. They are *indicators* of learning outcomes. Except in unusual cases, any one performance is just a sample of all the possible performances that would indicate an intended learning outcome. Chapters 2 and 3 cover this point in greater detail. For now, know that the purpose of the list in Figure 1.1 is to describe some of these performances, so you can recognize them as performances and as suitable for using rubrics, when they are appropriate indicators of your goals for student learning.

About the only kinds of schoolwork that do not function well with rubrics are questions with right or wrong answers. Test items or oral questions in class that have one clear correct answer are best assessed as right or wrong. However, even test items that have degrees of quality of performance, where you want to observe how appropriately, how completely, or how well a question was answered, can be assessed with rubrics.

Rubrics give structure to observations. Matching your observations of a student's work to the descriptions in the rubric averts the rush to judgment that can occur in classroom evaluation situations. Instead of *judging* the performance, the rubric *describes* the performance. The resulting judgment of quality based on a rubric therefore also contains within it a description of performance that can be used for feedback and teaching. This is different from a judgment of quality from a score or a grade arrived at without a rubric. Judgments without descriptions stop the action in a classroom.

Figure 1.1   Types of Performances That Can Be Assessed with Rubrics

Type of Performance	Examples
Processes • Physical skills • Use of equipment • Oral communication • Work habits	• Playing a musical instrument • Doing a forward roll • Preparing a slide for the microscope • Making a speech to the class • Reading aloud • Conversing in a foreign language • Working independently
Products • Constructed objects • Written essays, themes, reports, term papers • Other academic products that demonstrate understanding of concepts	• Wooden bookshelf • Set of welds • Handmade apron • Watercolor painting • Laboratory report • Term paper on theatrical conventions in Shakespeare's day • Written analysis of the effects of the Marshall Plan • Model or diagram of a structure (atom, flower, planetary system, etc.) • Concept map

What are the advantages and disadvantages of different types of rubrics?

Rubrics are usually categorized by two different aspects of their composition. One is whether the rubric treats the criteria one at a time or together. The other is whether the rubric is general and could be used with a family of similar tasks or is task-specific and only applicable to one assessment. Figure 1.2 describes the different types of rubrics and the advantages and disadvantages of each.

Analytic and holistic rubrics

Analytic rubrics describe work on each criterion separately. *Holistic rubrics* describe the work by applying all the criteria at the same time and enabling an overall judgment about the quality of the work. The top panel of Figure 1.2 defines analytic and holistic rubrics and lists advantages and disadvantages for each.

For most classroom purposes, analytic rubrics are best. Focusing on the criteria one at a time is better for instruction and better for formative assessment because students can see what aspects of their work need what kind of attention. Focusing on the criteria one at a time is good for any summative assessment (grading) that will also be used to make decisions about the future—for example, decisions about how to follow up on a unit or decisions about how to teach something next year.

One classroom purpose for which holistic rubrics are better than analytic rubrics is the situation in which students will not see the results of a final summative assessment and you will not really use the information for anything except a grade. Some high school final examinations fall into this category. Grading with rubrics is faster when there is only one decision to make, rather than a separate decision for each criterion.

On balance, for most classroom purposes I recommend analytic rubrics. Therefore, most of the examples in this book will be analytic rubrics. Before we leave holistic rubrics, however, I want to reemphasize the important point that *all the criteria* are used in holistic rubrics. You consider them together, but you don't boil down the evaluation to the old "excellent-good-fair-poor" kind of thinking along one general "judgment" dimension. True holistic rubrics are still rubrics; that is, they are based on criteria for good work and on observation of how the work meets those criteria.

Figure 1.2   Advantages and Disadvantages of Different Types of Rubrics

Type of Rubric	Definition	Advantages	Disadvantages
		Holistic or Analytic: One or Several Judgments?	
Analytic	• Each criterion (dimension, trait) is evaluated separately.	• Gives diagnostic information to teacher. • Gives formative feedback to students. • Easier to link to instruction than holistic rubrics. • Good for formative assessment; adaptable for summative assessment; if you need an overall score for grading, you can combine the scores.	• Takes more time to score than holistic rubrics. • Takes more time to achieve inter-rater reliability than with holistic rubrics.
Holistic	• All criteria (dimensions, traits) are evaluated simultaneously.	• Scoring is faster than with analytic rubrics. • Requires less time to achieve inter-rater reliability. • Good for summative assessment.	• Single overall score does not communicate information about what to do to improve. • Not good for formative assessment.

continued

Figure 1.2   Advantages and Disadvantages of Different Types of Rubrics (*continued*)

Type of Rubric	Definition	Advantages	Disadvantages
		Description of Performance: General or Task-Specific?	
General	• Description of work gives characteristics that apply to a whole family of tasks (e.g., writing, problem solving).	• Can share with students, explicitly linking assessment and instruction. • Reuse same rubrics with several tasks or assignments. • Supports learning by helping students see "good work" as bigger than one task. • Supports student self-evaluation. • Students can help construct general rubrics.	• Lower reliability at first than with task-specific rubrics. • Requires practice to apply well.
Task-Specific	• Description of work refers to the specific content of a particular task (e.g., gives an answer, specifies a conclusion).	• Teachers sometimes say using these makes scoring "easier." • Requires less time to achieve inter-rater reliability.	• Cannot share with students (would give away answers). • Need to write new rubrics for each task. • For open-ended tasks, good answers not listed in rubrics may be evaluated poorly.

Source: From *Assessment and Grading in Classrooms* (p. 201), by Susan M. Brookhart and Anthony J. Nitko, 2008, Upper Saddle River, NJ: Pearson Education. Copyright 2008 by Pearson Education. Reprinted with permission.

General and task-specific rubrics

General rubrics use criteria and descriptions of performance that *generalize* across (hence the name *general rubrics*), or can be used with, different tasks. The tasks all have to be instances of the same learning outcome—for example, writing or mathematics problem solving. The criteria point to aspects of the learning outcome and not to features of any one specific task (for example, criteria list characteristics of good problem solving and not features of the solution to a specific problem). The descriptions of performance are general, so students learn general qualities and not isolated, task-specific features (for example, the description might say all relevant information was used to solve the problem, not that the numbers of knives, forks, spoons, and guests were used to solve the problem). *Task-specific rubrics* are pretty well described by their name: They are rubrics that are specific to the performance task with which they are used. Task-specific rubrics contain the answers to a problem, or explain the reasoning students are supposed to use, or list facts and concepts students are supposed to mention. The bottom panel of Figure 1.2 defines general and task-specific rubrics and lists advantages and disadvantages for each.

Why use general rubrics? General rubrics have several advantages over task-specific rubrics. General rubrics

- Can be shared with students at the beginning of an assignment, to help them plan and monitor their own work.
- Can be used with many different tasks, focusing the students on the knowledge and skills they are developing over time.
- Describe student performance in terms that allow for many different paths to success.
- Focus the teacher on developing students' learning of skills instead of task completion.
- Do not need to be rewritten for every assignment.

Let's look more closely at the first two advantages.

Can be shared with students at the beginning of an assignment. General rubrics do not "give away answers" to questions. They do not contain any information that the students are supposed to be developing themselves. Instead, they contain descriptions like "Explanation of reasoning is clear and supported with appropriate details." Descriptions like this focus students on what their learning target is supposed to be (for example, explaining reasoning clearly, with appropriate supporting details). They clarify for students how to approach the assignment (for example, in solving the problem posed, I should make sure to explicitly focus on why I made the choices I did and be able to explain that). Therefore, over time general rubrics help students build up a concept of what it means to perform a skill well (for example, effective problem solving requires clear reasoning that I can explain and support).

Can be used with many different tasks. Because general rubrics focus students on the knowledge and skills they are learning rather than the particular task they are completing, they offer the best method I know for preventing the problem of "empty rubrics" that will be described in Chapter 2. Good general rubrics will, by definition, not be task directions in disguise, or counts of surface features, or evaluative rating scales.

Because general rubrics focus students on the knowledge and skills they are supposed to be acquiring, they can and should be used with any task that belongs to the whole domain of learning for those learning outcomes. Of course, you never have an opportunity to give students all of the potential tasks in a domain—you can't ask them to write every possible essay about characterization, solve every possible problem involving slope, design experiments involving every possible chemical solvent, or describe every political takeover that was the result of a power vacuum.

These sets of tasks all indicate important knowledge and skills, however, and they develop over time and with practice. Essay writing, problem solving, experimental design, and the analysis of political systems are each important skills in their respective disciplines. If the rubrics are the same each time a student does the same kind of work, the student will learn general qualities of good essay writing, problem solving, and so on. If the rubrics are different each time the student does the same kind of work, the student will not have an opportunity to see past the specific essay or problem. The general approach encourages students to think about building up general knowledge and skills rather than thinking about school learning in terms of getting individual assignments done.

Why use task-specific rubrics? Task-specific rubrics function as "scoring directions" for the person who is grading the work. Because they detail the elements to look for in a student's answer to a particular task, scoring students' responses with task-specific rubrics is lower-inference work than scoring students' responses with general rubrics. For this reason, it is faster to train raters to reach acceptable levels of scoring reliability using task-specific rubrics for large-scale assessment. Similarly, it is easier for teachers to apply task-specific rubrics consistently with a minimum of practice. General rubrics take longer to learn to apply well.

However, the reliability advantage is temporary (one can learn to apply general rubrics well), and it comes with a big downside. Obviously, task-specific rubrics are useful only for scoring. If students can't see the rubrics ahead of time, you can't share them with students, and therefore task-specific rubrics are not useful for formative assessment. That in itself is one good reason not to use them except for special purposes. Task-specific rubrics do not take advantage of the most powerful aspects of rubrics—their usefulness in helping students to conceptualize their learning targets and to monitor their own progress.

Why are rubrics important?

Rubrics are important because they clarify for students the qualities their work should have. This point is often expressed in terms of students understanding the learning target and criteria for success. For this reason, rubrics help teachers teach, they help coordinate instruction and assessment, and they help students learn.

Rubrics help teachers teach

To write or select rubrics, teachers need to focus on the criteria by which learning will be assessed. This focus on what you intend students to *learn* rather than what you intend to *teach* actually helps improve instruction. The common approach of "teaching things," as in "I taught the American Revolution" or "I taught factoring quadratic equations," is clear on content but not so clear on outcomes. Without clarity on outcomes, it's hard to know how much of various aspects of the content to teach. Rubrics help with clarity of both content and outcomes.

Really good rubrics help teachers avoid confusing the task or activity with the learning goal, and therefore confusing completion of the task with learning. Rubrics help keep teachers focused on criteria, not tasks. I have already discussed this point in the section about selecting criteria. Focusing rubrics on *learning* and not on *tasks* is the most important concept in this book. I will return to it over and over. It seems to be a difficult concept—or probably a more accurate statement is that focusing on tasks is so easy and so seductive that it becomes the path many busy teachers take. Penny-wise and pound-foolish, such an approach saves time in the short run by sacrificing learning in the long run.

Rubrics help coordinate instruction and assessment

Most rubrics should be designed for repeated use, over time, on several tasks. Students are given a rubric at the beginning of a unit of instruction or an episode of work. They tackle the work, receive feedback, practice, revise or do another task, continue to practice, and ultimately receive a grade—all using the same rubric as their description of the criteria and the quality levels that will demonstrate learning. This path to learning is much more cohesive than a string of assignments with related but different criteria.

Rubrics help students learn

The criteria and performance-level descriptions in rubrics help students understand what the desired performance is and what it looks like. Effective rubrics show students how they will know to what extent their performance passes muster on each criterion of importance, and if used formatively can also show students what their next steps should be to enhance the quality of their performance. This claim is backed by research at all grade levels and in different disciplines.

Several studies of student-generated criteria demonstrate that students can participate in defining and describing the qualities their work should have. Nancy Harris and Laura Kuehn (Higgins, Harris, & Kuehn, 1994) did research in their own team-taught classroom to see what sorts of criteria primary school students could generate for a "good project." They found that their students, in grades 1 and 2, were able to define criteria for group projects. At the beginning of the year, most of the criteria were about process (for example, the group members getting along with each other). In December, students were able to view examples of projects, and with continued brainstorming and discussion they began to see the importance of substantive criteria (for example, the information contained in the project). By the end of the year, about half the criteria students chose were about process and half were about product. This study shows us that students need to learn how to focus on learning—and, more important, that they can begin to do this as early as 1st grade.

Andrade, Du, and Wang (2008) investigated the effects of having 3rd and 4th graders read a model written assignment, generate their own list of criteria, and use rubrics to self-assess the quality of the written stories and essays they then produced. A comparison group brainstormed criteria and self-assessed their drafts but did not use the rubric. Controlling for previous writing ability, the group that used the rubrics for self-assessment wrote better overall, and specifically in the areas of ideas, organization, voice, and word choice. There were no differences between the groups in the areas of sentences and conventions, presumably areas of much previous drill for all young writers. Andrade, Du, and Mycek (2010) replicated these findings with students in 5th, 6th, and 7th grade, except that the rubric group's writing was evaluated as having higher quality on all six criteria.

Ross, Hoagaboam-Gray, and Rolheiser (2002) taught 5th and 6th grade students self-evaluation skills in mathematics, also using a method based on criteria. Their self-evaluation instruction involved four strategies: involving students in defining criteria, teaching them how to apply the criteria, giving them feedback on these self-evaluations against criteria, and helping them develop action plans based on the self-evaluations. Controlling for previous problem-solving ability, students who self-assessed using criteria outscored a comparison group at solving mathematics problems.

Ross and Starling (2008) used the same four-component self-assessment training, based on criteria, with secondary students in a 9th grade geography class. Students were learning to solve geography problems using global information systems (GIS) software, so the learning goals were about both accurate use of the software and applying it to real-world geography problems, including being able to explain their problem-solving strategies. Controlling for pretest computer self-efficacy (known to be important in technology learning), the treatment group outscored a comparison group on three different measures: production of a map using the software, a report explaining their problem-solving strategies, and an exam measuring knowledge of the mapping program. The largest difference was for the problem-solving explanations.

Hafner and Hafner (2003) investigated college biology students' use of rubrics for peer assessment and teacher assessment of a collaborative oral presentation. There were five criteria: organization and research, persuasiveness and logic of argument, collaboration, delivery and grammar, and creativity and originality. Originally the rubric was developed and then modified with discussion and involvement of students. For the study, the same rubric was used for a

> **SELF-REFLECTION**
>
> What evidence would it take to convince you that using rubrics with learning-based criteria in your classroom would enhance learning of content outcomes and improve students' learning skills as well? How can you get that evidence in your own classroom?

required course assignment three years in a row. The instructors were interested in finding out whether the information students gained from peer evaluation was accurate, whether it matched teacher input, and whether this accuracy was consistent across different years and classes. The short answer was yes. Students were able to accurately give feedback to their peers, their information matched that of their instructor, and this was the case for each class.

Summing up

This chapter has defined rubrics in terms of their two main components: criteria and descriptions of levels of performance. The main point about criteria is that they should be about learning outcomes, not aspects of the task itself. The main point about descriptions of levels of performance is that they should be descriptions, not evaluative statements. The "evaluation" aspect of assessment is accomplished by matching student work with the description, not by making immediate judgments. Finally, the chapter has presented some evidence that using this kind of rubric helps teachers teach and students learn, and it has invited you to pursue your own evidence, in your specific classroom and school context.

2

Common Misconceptions About Rubrics

This chapter starts with misconceptions about rubrics and then shows how the principles for writing or selecting effective rubrics overcome these problems. A couple of good counterexamples will, I think, show clearly how the principles for writing effective rubrics work.

I think it is likely that many misconceptions about rubrics stem from teachers' need to grab a tool—rubrics—and integrate the tool with what they already know and do about assessment, which is related mostly to grading. They may already have misconceptions about grading (Brookhart, 2011; O'Connor, 2011). Many well-meaning teachers use rubrics in ways that undermine students' learning. Many rubrics available on the Internet also exhibit these problems.

Confusing learning outcomes with tasks

Rubrics should not confuse the learning outcome to be assessed with the task used to assess it. Rubrics are not assignment directions set into chart format. The biggest mistake teachers make when they use rubrics with performance assessment is that they focus on the task, the product, and *not* the learning outcome or proficiency the task is supposed to get students to demonstrate. This has been my experience and has been documented by others as well.

Goldberg and Roswell (1999–2000) looked at 200 samples of classroom materials from eight elementary and three middle schools. Teachers were asked to select activities, lessons, unit plans, and assessments that they felt would give a "window" into their classrooms. Some of the teachers had had experience scoring for the Maryland School Performance Assessment Program (MSPAP) and some had not. The researchers were expecting that those with scoring experience would have created better scoring tools, including rubrics, than those who had not. However, they found that almost all of the teacher-created scoring tools included flaws that compromised their usefulness. These flaws included the following:

- Confounding the outcomes being measured [scoring more than one content-area skill at a time, without recognizing them as separate skills]
- Scoring for extraneous features (e.g., neatness, color, etc.)
- Scoring by counting up parts or components rather than by looking for evidence of proficiency in the outcome(s) being measured
- Scoring for things students have not been cued to do
- Scoring products rather than outcomes (p. 281)

Goldberg and Roswell (1999–2000) give a good example of what they meant by scoring products rather than outcomes. A social studies teacher intended to teach, and assess, students' understanding of two Maryland learning outcomes: "to examine or describe the processes people use for making and changing rules within the family, school, and community, . . . to propose rules that promote order and fairness in various situations" (p. 277). The teacher created a multipart performance task. First, students read the novel *Jumanji*, in which a board game goes out of control, and answered both literal and inferential questions. Then, in groups, the students brainstormed a list of other board games they were familiar with, invented a new board game, and participated in a tournament. Finally, they identified problems with the various games and revised them, and then wrote an advertisement to market their game. However, as Goldberg and Roswell point out, none of the questions or activities was about how and why people make rules for games.

Without a close analysis, this looks like a wonderful activity. It is cross-disciplinary (encompassing English language arts and social studies), engaging, and fun. It *could*, with some modification, actually teach and assess the intended social studies concepts. As it stands, however, it teaches and assesses reading comprehension (reading and answering questions about the novel, although not about the concept of people making rules), cooperative group skills (devising the games and the tournament), some problem-solving skills (diagnosing and revising the games), and communication skills (designing the advertisement).

These sorts of near-miss activities are often accompanied by miss-the-mark rubrics that assess the task, not the outcome. Using task-related criteria (Comprehension, Board Game, Tournament Participation, and Advertisement) would have resulted in a grade, but not one that gave any information about the social studies outcomes the grade was supposed to indicate. Had the task been modified so that the questions addressed the social studies concepts and the board game activity included a reflection or brainstorming session about the process of making rules, outcome-related criteria such as the following could have been used: Clear Explanation of the Rule-Making Process, Support for Explanation from Both the Novel and the Activity, and Demonstration of Order and Fairness of Rules in Revised Games.

The problem of focusing on the task or instructional activity and not on learning goals is not limited to performance assessment and selection of rubric criteria. It is common in teacher planning and assessment in general (Chappuis, Stiggins, Chappuis, & Arter, 2012). This problem of confusing a task with a learning goal is highlighted in the selection of rubric criteria, however, because of the huge temptation to align the criteria to the task instead of the learning goal and because of the existence of so many near-miss—engaging but "empty" (Goldberg & Roswell, 1999–2000, p. 276)—classroom performance tasks. In fact, many performance tasks and their associated rubrics are a lot more empty than the board game example. I have chosen this "near-miss" example to make the point about rubrics indicating learning, not task completion, precisely because it looks so good. It is not a straw man to knock down.

Not focusing beyond tasks to intended learning outcomes is an error on two levels. First, students really will think that what you ask them to *do* exemplifies what you want them to *learn*. Therefore, the task should be a "performance of understanding" (Moss & Brookhart, 2012) and not a near miss. Near miss tasks cheat students out of learning opportunities and out of opportunities to conceptualize what it is that they are supposed to be learning. Second, task-based, as opposed to learning-based, criteria do not yield the kind of information you and your students need to support future learning. Instead, they yield information about what was *done,* and they stop the action—the task, after all, is completed. The resulting information is more about work habits, following directions, and being a "good student" than it is about learning. The opportunity to foster and then gauge learning is missed.

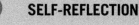

SELF-REFLECTION

Think about a performance assessment that you have used and scored with rubrics. Were the criteria in the rubrics about the task or about the learning outcomes the task was intended to have students demonstrate? Do the task and rubric criteria need modification, and if so, what would that look like?

This is not to say we don't want students to learn how to follow directions or give them tools to help with that. Of course we do. Often a checklist or a rating scale (see Chapter 7) can be used for the task-related aspects of the assignment. A checklist can help students judge the completeness of their work so they know they are turning in what is required and are developing work habits in the process. In contrast, the learning-focused rubric helps you and your students gauge what was *learned* in the doing of the task.

Confusing rubrics with requirements or quantities

Rubrics are not about the requirements for the assignment, nor are they about counting things. As the previous section showed, a very seductive but poor use for rubrics is to codify the directions for an assignment into a chart that lists the features of the task (for example, "cover page") and the number or kind of required elements for each feature. Students then comply with the rubrics to earn points. This is a grade-focused, not a learning-focused, way to use rubrics. I say that it is "seductive" because it works, in the short run, to produce compliant students who complete their assignments for the purpose of getting the grade they want. Teachers who don't think beyond this to whether the compliance gives evidence of learning can easily get stuck in this habit. I know some teachers who use this kind of "rubric" for everything.

Figure 2.1 shows what unfortunately is a quite common type of rubric. Many of you may recognize the assignment. Students, typically in pairs or groups, are assigned to make a poster with facts about a topic under study. I have seen versions of this assignment done with states in the United States (as in this example), continents, Canadian provinces, planets, and elements on the periodic table. Sometimes students can choose the state, continent, or what have you, and sometimes it is assigned.

Teachers usually assume that the students are "learning" the facts as they look them up, but the poster assignment gives no evidence of this. It only gives evidence that students can look up a state in an encyclopedia or on the Internet and copy information about it. The assignment is really about decorating the classroom or hallway and having

Figure 2.1   Example of a Poor "Rubric"

My State Poster				
	4	**3**	**2**	**1**
Facts	The poster includes at least 6 facts about the state and is interesting to read.	The poster includes 4–5 facts about the state and is interesting to read.	The poster includes at least 2–3 facts about the state.	Several facts are missing.
Graphics	All graphics are related to the topic and make it easier to understand.	One graphic is not related to the topic.	Two graphics are not related to the topic.	Graphics do not relate to the topic.
Neatness	The poster is exceptionally attractive in terms of design, layout, and neatness.	The poster is attractive in terms of design, layout, and neatness.	The poster is acceptably attractive, although it may be a bit messy.	The poster is messy or very poorly designed.
Grammar	There are no mistakes in grammar, punctuation, or spelling.	There are 1–2 mistakes in grammar, punctuation, or spelling.	There are 3–4 mistakes in grammar, punctuation, or spelling.	There are more than 4 mistakes in grammar, punctuation, or spelling.

fun with facts. This is a good example of an "empty" task that does not give students opportunities to demonstrate the intended learning outcomes.

The best way to assess recall of facts is with a simple test or quiz. Making a poster might be an instructional activity to help students get ready for the test. Or perhaps there are more important uses of instructional and assessment time for a unit on the states than memorizing sets of facts about them. That depends on the district curriculum and state standards. At any rate, I am going to use the rubric for this common task to illustrate what *not* to do. I have met many teachers who really do think rubrics like the one in Figure 2.1 are good for students. Not so!

With these "rubrics," the assignment really doesn't need any more directions except perhaps "Work with a partner, and pick a state." These rubrics are really more like a checklist for students to use, listing desired attributes of the task, not the learning it is designed to represent. The posters should have six facts, each illustrated with a graphic, and they should be neat and use correct grammar. There is nothing wrong with checking for this, and the teacher could create a tool if she wished. The resulting checklist could be used for self-assessment of the completeness of the poster activity:

My state poster
_____ Has six facts.
_____ Has a picture related to each fact.
_____ Is neat.
_____ Uses correct grammar.

Whether the students could recall the facts they were supposed to know would be assessed separately, with a quiz.

The My State Poster rubric illustrates another common misconception about the descriptions of performance along the continuum of quality for each criterion. Rarely is a count the best way to distinguish levels of quality of criteria, and if it is, the criteria are likely related to work habits (for example, counting how often a student completes homework). Chapter 7 discusses how to build rating scales with frequency levels as indicators of work habits and other learning skills.

Occasionally an academic learning goal is best measured with counts (for example, counting the number of errors in a keyboarding passage). But most of the time, the best way to describe levels of quality is with substantive descriptions. The poster rubric has a glimmer of that in the Level 4 description for graphics: "All graphics are related to the topic and make it easier to understand." The quality of an illustration making something easier to understand is a substantive one. But this aspect of the graphics is not carried through in parallel form for the other levels (for example, "Graphics are included but do not add to understanding," "Graphics are included but are confusing," and so on). Instead, the descriptions turn into counts. Counts are used for the criteria of facts and grammar as well. The only criterion with substantive descriptions of performance at each level is neatness.

I have also seen versions of the poster assignment that have "criteria" for each of the intended facts. For example, a class was assigned to make posters about a chosen Native American group, and the criteria on the rubric were Name of the Group, Type of Dwelling, Location, Dress, Food, and Neatness/Mechanics/Creativity.

Once again, let me be clear that I have nothing against posters and nothing against facts. What is at issue here is the use of task-based (rather than learning-based) rubrics that count or enumerate aspects of the directions students are expected to follow. The resulting "grade" is an evaluation of compliance, not of learning. Students could "score" top points on these rubrics and, in fact, understand nothing except how to make a neat poster. Students can also "score" top points on these rubrics and understand a lot. You don't know, and your rubrics can't tell you. That's a problem.

In summary, rubrics with criteria that are about the task—with descriptions of performance that amount to checklists for directions—assess compliance and not learning. Rubrics with counts instead of quality descriptions assess the existence of something and not its quality. Most of the time this also means the intended learning outcome is not assessed.

Confusing rubrics with evaluative rating scales

Another common problem with rubrics happens when teachers identify the criteria to be evaluated but then add a rating scale for each and call it a "rubric." These kinds of documents abound in schools and on the Internet. Another version of this is to use a numerical scale for each criterion, with higher numbers usually intended to mean better work. Yet another way that rating scales masquerade as rubrics is in graphic scales that use such images as a frowny face, a straight face, and a smiley face.

For example, a high school social studies teacher asked his students to summarize their lecture notes for a unit of study by creating presentation slides. Each group showed their slides to the class. This actually would be a great review activity. Students would work together and would have to talk about the material in order to decide what should go into their presentation slides. They would rehearse and review the facts and concepts as they did this, and again as they presented their work and listened to the presentations of others. This instructional activity, however, came with a rubric. There were three criteria: Content, Images/Slides, and Oral Presentation, each with scales consisting of Excellent, Good, Fair, and Poor, which translated quickly into *A*, *B*, *C*, and *D* grades.

SELF-REFLECTION

Were you familiar with the argument against rubrics that merely summarize the requirements of the task, as opposed to rubrics that describe evidence of learning? If your school has begun to tackle this issue, what have been the results? If the argument is new to you, what do you think about this issue now?

In summary, rubrics with evaluative scales instead of descriptive scales assess work quality by "grading" it and therefore miss the main advantage of rubrics. The main function of rubrics is to allow you to match the performance to a description rather than immediately judge it. This is hugely important. What is at issue is the nature of the evidence. The rubric description is the bridge between what you see (the student work, the evidence) and the judgment of learning. If you're not going to take advantage of that main function, you might as well just go back to the old-fashioned way of marking a grade on a paper without explanation.

Summing up

This chapter took a brief look at some common misconceptions about rubrics to sharpen your "radar" so that you can avoid these pitfalls in rubrics you write yourself or with your students. In the next chapter you will learn how to write or select effective rubrics for use in your classroom.

3

Writing or Selecting Effective Rubrics

One purpose of this chapter is to help you write—alone, with colleagues, or with your students—rubrics that will support learning in your classroom. Another purpose is to help you become a savvy consumer of the rubric resources that abound. If you know how to write effective rubrics, you can sometimes save time by finding and using existing ones. You may find useful rubrics that you can use as is, or fairly good ones that you can revise and adopt for your purposes. And of course, if you know how effective rubrics are written, you can dismiss the numerous ineffective ones you will find. Whether you are writing your own rubrics or selecting rubrics written by others to adapt for your own use, focus on their two main defining aspects: the criteria and the descriptions of levels of performance.

How to decide on appropriate criteria

The first questions to ask when you are writing a rubric, selecting a rubric, or co-constructing a rubric with students are these: What are the criteria for good work on the task that the rubric is to assess? What should a student, peer, or teacher be looking for? One of the most valuable aspects of using rubrics is that these qualities are named and described. They become the target students will aim for.

Select as criteria the most appropriate and important aspects of the work given what the task is supposed to assess. These should not, generally, be characteristics of the task itself (for example, Cover, Report on Famous Person, Visuals, References), but rather characteristics of the learning outcome the task is supposed to indicate (for example, Selection of Subject, Analysis of Famous Person's Contribution to History, Support with Appropriate Historical Facts and Reasoning). Such criteria support learning because they describe qualities that you and the students should look for as evidence of students' learning.

Appropriateness is the most important "criterion for criteria," if you will; that is, it is the most important property or characteristic that criteria for effective rubrics should possess. But it's not the only one. To be useful and effective for rubrics, the criteria you choose also need to be definable and observable. They should also be different from one another, so that they can be appraised separately, and yet as a group define a set of characteristics that, taken together, describe performance in a complete enough manner to match the description of learning in the standard or instructional goal. Finally, criteria should be characteristics that can vary along a quality continuum from high to low, so you can write meaningful performance-level descriptions. Figure 3.1 summarizes the characteristics you want in a set of criteria for rubrics for a performance.

There will be additional characteristics "in the background"—Sadler (1989) called these "latent criteria"—that students have already mastered or that are not the main focus of an assignment. For example, in a high school science laboratory report, students will use sentencing skills that they learned in early elementary school. "Sentencing skills" operate in the background, are important in an overall sense for writing good laboratory reports, but are not likely to be part of the rubric used to evaluate the reports. In most cases, appropriate criteria for a high school laboratory report would have to do with understanding the science content, understanding the inquiry process and scientific reasoning, and skillfully communicating findings via a conventional laboratory report. Effective rubrics do not list all possible criteria; they list the *right* criteria for the assessment's purpose.

To choose criteria, start with your intended learning outcome, as stated in the standard or instructional goal you are intending to assess. Ask yourself this question:

The Criterion Question: What *characteristics of student work* would give *evidence* for student learning of the knowledge or skills specified in this standard (or instructional goal)?

Figure 3.1   Desired Characteristics of Criteria for Classroom Rubrics

Characteristics The criteria are . . .	Explanation
Appropriate	Each criterion represents an aspect of a standard, curricular goal, or instructional goal or objective that students are intended to learn.
Definable	Each criterion has a clear, agreed-upon meaning that both students and teachers understand.
Observable	Each criterion describes a quality in the performance that can be perceived (seen or heard, usually) by someone other than the person performing.
Distinct from one another	Each criterion identifies a separate aspect of the learning outcomes the performance is intended to assess.
Complete	All the criteria together describe the whole of the learning outcomes the performance is intended to assess.
Able to support descriptions along a continuum of quality	Each criterion can be described over a range of performance levels.

For most standards and instructional goals, the answers to this question will be characteristics that could be elements of student work on more than one task. For example, if students are supposed to be able to "cite textual evidence to support analysis of what the text says explicitly as well as inferences drawn from the text" (CCSSI ELA Standard RL.8.1), then they should be able to do that in a variety of different tasks. Students might read a passage and then answer a question or set of questions in writing. They might read a passage and participate in a discussion with peers. They might read a passage and explain what it meant to a fictional younger student. They might read a passage and make a list of literal and inferential conclusions they could draw from the reading. They might use this skill in a more complex task, like comparing and contrasting two texts. In addition, any of these kinds of tasks might be based on different passages.

The result is a huge number of potential tasks, and you want the characteristics of performance that give evidence applicable to all potential tasks by which students could demonstrate how well they have learned this skill. In other words, you want criteria that are appropriate to the learning common to all the tasks.

How to write performance-level descriptions

The most important aspect of the levels is that performance be *described*, with language that depicts what one would observe in the work rather than the quality conclusions one would draw. As I noted in Chapter 2, a common misconception I see regarding rubrics is that after criteria are identified, they are given evaluative scales (for example, Excellent, Good, Fair, Poor). These are not rubrics; they are old-fashioned grading scales. Descriptions of performance levels can be general, describing a whole family of tasks (for example, "Uses an appropriate solution strategy"), or task-specific (for example, "Uses the equation $2x + 5 = 15$"). Decide whether you need general or task-specific descriptions of performance levels (see Figure 1.2); in most cases, general descriptions are preferred.

A second aspect of levels of performance that needs to be decided is how many levels there should be. The best answer to this question is the conceptual answer: Use as many levels as you can describe in terms of meaningful differences in performance quality. For some simple tasks, this will be two levels: Acceptable and Redo, or Mastery and Not Yet.

In practice, you don't want to end up with an overabundance of uncoordinated evaluation results that will be difficult to summarize. And often there are several different ways you could describe the continuum of performance quality, using more or fewer levels. Therefore I recommend that you choose a number of levels that will coordinate with your requirements for grading (Brookhart, 1999, 2011), if possible. For many classrooms, this means four (for example, Advanced, Proficient, Basic, Below Basic) or five (for example, *A, B, C, D, F*) levels. If it is not possible to coordinate the number of levels with practical grading constraints, rather than violating the criteria and their descriptions, design a rubric that is faithful to the task and its quality criteria, and then figure out a way to include it in a summary grade if that is needed (see Chapter 11).

Once you have decided on the number of levels, you need a description of performance quality for each level of each criterion. A common way to write these descriptions is to begin with the performance level you intend for most students to reach (for example, Proficient), describe that, and then adjust the remaining descriptions from there—backing off (for example, for Basic and Below Basic) or building up (for example, for Advanced). Another common way is to start with the top category (for example, *A*), describe that, and then back off (for example, for *B, C, D, F*). These methods illustrate two different approaches to assessment. In a standards-based grading context, Advanced is supposed to be described by achievement above and beyond what is expected. In a traditional grading context, often the *A* is what students are aiming for. Ask yourself this question:

> **The Performance Description Question:** What does student work look like at each level of quality, from high to low, on this criterion?

Whether you begin with the Proficient category or the top category for a criterion, you don't write four or five completely different descriptions for the different levels of performance. You describe a continuum of levels of performance quality. These levels should be distinguishable. You should be able to describe what is different from one level to the next and to illustrate those descriptions with examples of students' work. Figure 3.2 summarizes desired characteristics for descriptions of levels of performance.

Describe student performance in terms that allow for many different paths to success. Good general rubrics do not overly constrain or stifle students. Chapman and Inman (2009) report this story about a 5th grader:

> The eleven-year old had a science assignment to complete as homework. Her parent, attempting to help, offered several suggestions for enhancing the project. The child's response to each suggestion was: "No, that's not on the rubric. Here's the rubric, Mother. This is all we're supposed to do." (p. 198)

Chapman and Inman use this story to argue that rubrics constrain creativity and metacognitive development. I disagree. Rather, *bad* rubrics constrain creativity and metacognitive development. These rubrics were the "directions" type described in Chapter 2. The authors described them as a chart in which each cell "includes specific elements that are either present or absent" (p. 198). In terms of my definition of rubrics, there were no descriptions of levels of performance quality on the criteria. These were, in fact, checklists dressed up as rubrics.

Choose the words in your performance-level descriptions carefully. Performance-level descriptions should, as the name implies, *describe* student performance at all levels

Figure 3.2   Desired Characteristics of Descriptions of Levels of Performance for Classroom Rubrics

Characteristics The descriptions of levels of performance are . . .	Explanation
Descriptive	Performance is described in terms of what is observed in the work.
Clear	Both students and teachers understand what the descriptions mean.
Cover the whole range of performance	Performance is described from one extreme of the continuum of quality to another for each criterion.
Distinguish among levels	Performance descriptions are different enough from level to level that work can be categorized unambiguously. It should be possible to match examples of work to performance descriptions at each level.
Center the target performance (acceptable, mastery, passing) at the appropriate level	The description of performance at the level expected by the standard, curriculum goal, or lesson objective is placed at the intended level on the rubric.
Feature parallel descriptions from level to level	Performance descriptions at each level of the continuum for a given standard describe different quality levels for the same aspects of the work.

of a continuum of performance. Evaluative terms (*excellent, good, fair, poor,* and the like) are not used. The continuum should represent realistic expectations for the content and grade level. Within that limit, descriptions should include all possible levels, including, for example, a bottom level that is completely off target, even if no student is expected to produce work at that level. The descriptions should be appropriate for the level they are describing. For example, the description of performance at the Proficient level in standards-based rubrics should match the level of intended accomplishment written in the standard, goal, or objective.

The descriptions should be clear and based on the same elements of performance from level to level. For example, consider the criterion Identifies the Problem in a mathematics problem-solving rubric. If part of the description of proficiency is that a student "states the problem in terms of its mathematical requirements," then each level of that criterion should have a description of the way students do that. Lesser instances of this aspect of performance might be described like this: "States the problem but does not use mathematical language" and "Does not state the problem."

Two general approaches to designing rubrics

There are two main approaches to designing rubrics: top-down and bottom-up (Nitko & Brookhart, 2011). The two methods do not necessarily lead to the same rubrics. Select the method that best suits your purposes. For work involving newly introduced concepts and skills, it is better to use the top-down approach and then familiarize the students with rubrics by having them look at samples of work using the criteria and levels provided. This will help the students develop their conceptions of quality work. Student co-construction of rubrics using a bottom-up approach works best for general learning outcomes with which students are already somewhat familiar.

Top-down approach

A top-down approach is deductive. It starts with a conceptual framework that describes the content and performance you will be assessing. Use the top-down approach when your curriculum or standards have clearly defined the intended content and performance. Here are the steps in the top-down approach:

1. *Create (or adapt from an existing source) a conceptual framework for achievement.* This should include a description of the intended achievement (e.g., what is good narrative writing?) and an outline of the qualities that you intend to teach and to ask students to demonstrate (the achievement dimensions or criteria). The outline should describe the continuum of performance for each criterion.
2. *Write general scoring rubrics using these dimensions and performance levels.* To do this, organize the criteria either analytically (one scale for each criterion) or holistically (one scale considering all criteria simultaneously) and write descriptions for performance at each level. The general rubrics can

and should be shared with students. For example, if you are constructing mathematical problem-solving rubrics and one of the criteria is "mathematical content knowledge," the general rubrics may say "problem solution shows understanding of major mathematical concepts and principles." Having students recognize the mathematical concepts and principles (e.g., "I know this problem involves the relationships among distance, rate, and time, and those are the major concepts") is part of the learning.

3. *For teacher scoring, you may adapt the general scoring rubrics for the specific learning goal for the performance you will be scoring.* For example, if the general rubrics say, "Problem solution shows understanding of major mathematical concepts and principles," to focus your scoring you might say, "Problem solution shows understanding of the relationships among distance, rate, and time."

4. *In either case (whether the rubrics remain general or are adapted to more specific learning goals), use the rubrics to assess several students' performances, and adapt them as needed for final use.* (Nitko & Brookhart, 2011, pp. 267–268)

Bottom-up approach

A bottom-up approach is inductive. It starts with samples of student work and uses them to create a framework for assessment. Use the bottom-up approach when you are still defining the descriptions of content and performance or when you want to involve students in creating the means of their own assessment. Here are the steps in the bottom-up approach:

1. *Get a dozen or more copies of students' work.* This student work should all be relevant to the kind of performance for which you are building rubrics (e.g., mathematics problem solving). However, if possible they should be from several different tasks (Arter & Chappuis, 2006). The reason for this is that you want the rubrics to reflect the content and performance descriptions for the general learning outcomes, not any particular task (e.g., not any one particular mathematics problem).

2. *Sort, or have students sort, the work into three piles: high, medium, and low quality work.* This is the reason that students need to be somewhat familiar with the concepts and skills. If they are not, their sorting may resort to

surface-level skills like neatness and format rather than the quality of the thinking and demonstration of skills.

3. *Write, or have students write, specific descriptions of why each piece of work is categorized as it is.* Be specific; for example, instead of saying that the problem was solved incorrectly, say what was done and why: the solution used irrelevant information, or the problem was approached as a volume problem when it was an area problem, or whatever.

4. *Compare and contrast the descriptions of work and extract criteria or dimensions.* For example, if there are several descriptions of students using relevant and irrelevant information, identifying relevant information in the problem may emerge as a dimension.

5. *For each of the criteria identified in step 4, write descriptions of quality along the dimensions, for as many levels as needed.* You may use three categories as you did for the sorting, or you may use four, five, or six, depending on how many distinctions are useful to make and/or how many levels you need for grading or other purposes. (Nitko & Brookhart, 2011, p. 268)

Choosing criteria and writing performance-level descriptions: A silly example

Let's use a silly example for our first illustration of writing a rubric. Suppose you were teaching an acting class and you wanted your students to be able to laugh on cue. Think of some television shows or movies you have seen where the actors needed to do this. Laughing is a performance, and it's a process as opposed to a product. You would show your students clips of actors laughing: the Joker in a Batman film or Santa Claus in a Christmas movie, perhaps. You would ask them to practice laughing themselves. And you would, at some point, help them develop criteria for their "work" that they could use to define, develop, and eventually evaluate it. In fact, that might be a fun exercise to do with colleagues.

One set of criteria for laughing might be Volume, Duration, and Body Involvement. These are not the only possible criteria. A colleague and I experimented with others. Figure 3.3 shows how we wrote descriptions of levels of performance for these criteria for a rubric for laughing. Don't laugh (pun intended!), but it may surprise you to learn that the descriptions in this rubric are not all of the same sort, and that we crafted them specifically to be able to illustrate different levels of inferences that descriptions require you to make.

Figure 3.3   Rubric for Laughing

Criteria	Performance Levels			
	Level 4 Guffaw	**Level 3** Laugh	**Level 2** Giggle	**Level 1** Chuckle
Volume	Laughter is loud enough to call attention to itself and annoy people. OR Laughter is so intense there is no noise at all.	Laughter is loud, verging on impolite, and can be heard by anyone in the room.	Laughter is of a polite, medium volume and can be heard by those in the immediate vicinity.	Laughter is audible to those standing nearby.
Duration	Laughter is self-sustaining, perpetuating itself until it becomes necessary for the laugher or a friend to intentionally put a stop to it.	Laughter is repeated several times, perhaps waning and then gathering strength again, as if the laugher is reimagining what is funny.	Laughter trills, cackles, or giggles for at least one repeat cycle.	Laughter is a brief snort, hoot, chortle, or chuckle.
Body Involvement	The whole body is involved, which may include (but is not limited to) shoulder rolls, head bobbling, whole-body shaking, doubling over, or falling down.	Cheeks scrunch up. At least one body part besides the face moves; perhaps the shoulders roll or the head is thrown back.	Lips open, face smiles.	Lips may open or may stay closed.

Some of the descriptions in this rubric are *low-inference*, which means that the observer does not have to draw a conclusion or make any surmises about what the observation might mean. "Lips open" is a low-inference description. Most people observing the same person laughing would agree on whether the person's lips were open or not. Notice that even this description is not totally objective: How far apart do lips have to be before they are described as "open"? Silly, sure, but it's easier to make this point with laughing lips than with aspects of student work about which a teacher may hold longstanding opinions. The point of a description is it makes you *look* and report what you *see*, not your opinion about it.

Some of the descriptions in this rubric are *high-inference*, which means that the observer has to draw a conclusion or make a surmise about what is observed. For example, "laughter is loud" is fairly low-inference, but "verging on impolite" is high-inference. Different people might draw different conclusions about how loud laughter has to be before it verges on impolite.

It would be easy to say just don't use descriptions that require inferences, but unfortunately that is too easy. *Aim for the lowest-inference descriptors that you can use and still accomplish your purpose of assessing important qualities.* As you do this, you will find that most descriptions you use will require some level of inference, even when they appear to be objective. For example, a common description of the Proficient level for a Grammar and Usage criterion for written reports would read something like "Few errors in grammar and usage, and errors do not interfere with meaning." There are inferences to be made. How few is few? How muddled does a sentence have to be before its meaning is unclear to a reader?

The important point here is that leaving descriptions open to professional judgment —to making some inferences—is better than locking things down with overly rigid descriptions. Don't be tempted to make everything so low-inference (for example, "three errors in grammar") that you don't leave room for good judgment. The role of the descriptions is interpreting the criteria along a continuum of quality. Three small errors in grammar may characterize an essay that exhibits much more complex and sophisticated English communication than an essay that has only one but that doesn't attempt much beyond short, simple sentences. Aha! I hope you are thinking already that declaring writing "complex" and "sophisticated" also requires making inferences. If so, point made. There is no way to make critical thinking about students' demonstration of what they know and can do completely inference-free. If you try, you end up with rubrics that are pretty trivial, as we explored in Chapter 2.

Choosing criteria and writing performance-level descriptions: A real example

This example illustrates the top-down method, and it also illustrates the importance of drafting and revising rubrics when you design them. Courtney Kovatch had taught her 3rd graders at West Hills Primary School in Kittanning, Pennsylvania, a science unit on habitats and life cycles of animals. As part of that unit, she asked students to work in pairs to do animal life-cycle research and then present their findings on a poster and orally as a report to the class.

First-draft rubric. Ms. Kovatch created a rubric for the life-cycle project. She developed her conceptual framework for achievement, using as criteria characteristics she wanted to see in the finished work. She gave the students the rubric at the same time she gave the assignment. She and the students discussed the rubric before beginning work and during work on the project. They did a class example, and then the pairs used the rubric for self-assessment and revision before their project was due. The self-assessment was productive for the students; most were able to improve their posters—and describe those improvements—before turning in their finished work.

The rubric makes an excellent example because it has many strong points, and yet there are clear places where revision would improve it. Figure 3.4 presents the first draft of the rubric.

I selected this example because there is a lot to work with here. Some readers may be already launching into a critique, and we'll get there, but please notice that you can tell by reading the descriptions that the teacher had modeled at least some of her thinking after soundly designed rubrics. I think it's instructive to see how these rubrics can be improved, and I thank Ms. Kovatch for allowing us all to learn from her example.

The rubric in Figure 3.4 is a true rubric—that is, it has criteria and performance-level descriptions. Several of the criteria do address the question: What *characteristics of student work* would give *evidence* for student learning of the knowledge or skills specified in this standard (or instructional goal)? Specifically, if the instructional goal was for students to know that animals have life cycles and to be able to find out, via research, about the life cycle of an animal, then three of the criteria in particular seem relevant: Order (an important concept in any "cycle"), Illustrations (important for communicating understanding), and Description of Life-Cycle Stages. Similarly, the performance-level descriptions begin to answer the question: What does student work look like at each level of quality, from high to low, on this criterion? Finally, Ms. Kovatch had given some thought to the weighting of the criteria and had made Illustrations and Description

Figure 3.4   First Draft of Life-Cycle Project Rubric

	6 Points	4 Points	2 Points	0 Points
Title of Poster		Title is evident on poster, correctly spelled and capitalized.	Title is on poster, but with errors or it is hard to read.	No title or heading.
Order of Life-Cycle Stages		All the stages of the life cycle are in the correct order. Stages are correctly labeled.	One or more stages of the life cycle are in the wrong order.	Not included.
Illustrations of Life-Cycle Stages	Illustrations of each stage are evident.	One or two illustrations of the life-cycle stages are missing.	More than 2 illustrations of the life-cycle stages are missing.	Not included.
Description of Life-Cycle Stages	Stages are described with at least 2 details.	Stages are described with one detail. One or more stage is missing.	Stages are incomplete or missing. Stages have one or zero supporting details.	Not included.
Overall Appearance of Poster		Poster is very neat and organized. Title and all sentences have correct spelling, capitalization, and punctuation.	Poster is somewhat neat and organized. Some correct spelling, punctuation, and capitalization. Poster shows signs of little effort.	Poster is messy, many errors, not colored, or unfinished. Poster shows no signs of effort.

Source: Used with permission from Courtney Kovatch, 3rd grade teacher, West Hills Primary School, Kittanning, PA.

of Life-Cycle Stages more important than the other criteria by allocating more points to them. Given her intended learning outcome, these were the appropriate criteria to weight more heavily.

Revising the rubric. This rubric would be more effective if it were edited to address the following points:

- Remove format criteria from the rubric and deal with them as work-habits issues.
- Replace points with proficiency levels.
- Edit performance-level descriptions to include fewer counts and more substantive statements.

The results would be more like the rubric in Figure 3.5.

Criteria. The science instructional goal was for students to know that animals have life cycles and to be able to find out, via research, about the life cycle of an animal. Three of the criteria match the goal, and they are retained in the revised version. They could also have been collapsed into one (Demonstrates Understanding of the Life Cycle of the Animal). In the original version, two of the criteria (Title and Overall Appearance) were about format and English mechanics (capitalization, punctuation), with some effort and work habits (neatness, "effort") thrown in. These are not part of science achievement.

The English mechanics could have been assessed and graded separately, and the results used to inform the students' English grades, but that was not what the teacher intended here. Teachers who wish to do that could assess English mechanics with a separate criterion. That criterion, however, should be about mechanics. Neatness and "effort" would be assessed as work habits and reported separately from the academic achievement grade.

Ms. Kovatch did not really intend to assess English mechanics. Those criteria were in the rubric simply because she thought they were important. A checklist that included neatness, title, capitalization, punctuation, and the like would have been a good way to handle that without mixing nonscience achievement into the science grade. She could have made a checklist for student self- or peer evaluation and required students to sign off on their work (or their peers' work) before turning it in. Some teachers are surprised that when you remove work habits from the grade, students still turn in neat work. In fact, that is usually what happens. Is every poster a Rembrandt? No, but work is no less neat than it would have been under the "grade neatness" system, especially if checklists or other aids are used. And a big gain is made, because the project grade more accurately reflects the learning standard or goal it was intended to assess.

Figure 3.5   Revised Version of Life-Cycle Project Rubric

	Advanced	Proficient	Nearing Proficient	Novice
Order of Life-Cycle Stages		All the stages of the life cycle are in the correct order and correctly labeled.	One or more stages of the life cycle are in the wrong order.	No order is specified, or order is incorrect.
Illustrations of Life-Cycle Stages	Each stage has an illustration that gives an especially clear or detailed view about what happens to the animal then.	Each stage has an illustration that helps show what happens to the animal then.	Some stage illustrations do not show what happens to the animal then.	Illustrations do not help show what happens to the animal during its life cycle.
Description of Life-Cycle Stages	Stages are described accurately. Descriptions are especially complete and detailed.	Stages are described accurately.	Stages are described with some inaccurate or incomplete information.	No stages are described, or stages are described inaccurately.

Performance levels. The teacher's original intent was to add up the points and take a percentage grade, a common approach used in her school. For this intention, weighting the title, order, and overall appearance criteria 4 points instead of 6 made sense. For reasons that are discussed more thoroughly in Chapter 10, using points and percentages for grading with rubrics is not recommended. Doing so removes some of the observation and judgment of work that is a strength of rubrics, and often the results do not match actual student performance and achievement. The revised rubrics use proficiency-level descriptions (Advanced, Proficient, Nearing Proficient, and Novice) instead of points. Then the descriptions can be written to those levels. Notice that one of the criteria, Order of Life-Cycle Stages, does not have an Advanced level. Knowing the order of an organism's life-cycle stages is a characteristic of proficiency. Any advanced understanding about the life cycle would be expressed in the descriptions and illustrations.

Descriptions of performance at each level. Several "wordsmithing" revisions have been made in the descriptions of performance at each level from Figure 3.4 to Figure 3.5. First, numerical counts ("one stage," "one detail") are replaced with substantive judgments. This revision actually makes the assessment more accurate, not less accurate, as you might think. Different animals have different life cycles, and some stages and details are more important than others. The revised descriptions require figuring out how clearly the students' descriptions show their understanding of the research they have done, rather than the number of facts they copied. This, in turn, will make for a more accurate assessment of students' understandings of animal life cycles. And it will discourage students from copying facts instead of interpreting what they learned by reading the facts.

SELF-REFLECTION

Do you sometimes use rubrics that are more about assignment directions than evidence of learning? If you do, try to revise your rubrics in a similar manner to the way we revised the Life-Cycle Project rubric. Even better, work with a colleague, so you can discuss the issues raised in this chapter as you revise.

Second, there is space for describing performance at an Advanced level—that is, beyond that necessary for simply doing what was required. Because students have the rubrics ahead of time, they know that they can include extra-detailed, more complex descriptions if they are able. The first draft of the rubric provided no reason for students to do anything above or beyond listing stages in their chosen animal's life cycle, copying two facts about each stage, and using some sort of illustration. The revised rubric allows teachers and students to judge how deeply students delve into the subject, and it encourages delving.

Summing up

The chapter provided suggestions for choosing criteria and writing descriptions of levels of performance, intended to help you write rubrics or adapt rubrics that you find on the Internet or in other resources. Chapters 4, 5, and 6 discuss three kinds of rubrics that are effective for teaching and learning, depending on your purpose.

4

General Rubrics for Fundamental Skills

General rubrics are particularly useful for fundamental skills that develop over time. Writing and mathematics problem solving are two examples. This chapter begins by describing general rubrics for these skills. In both cases, the disciplines have agreed on the skills involved. In writing, the 6+1 Trait Writing rubrics have become widely accepted as clear statements of what good writing looks like. More recently, agreement has begun to converge in the field of mathematics on what good problem solving looks like, and although there are many math problem-solving rubrics, they tend to be more alike than different. Generally accepted criteria for mathematics problem solving have included strategic knowledge and mathematical communication since at least 1989, when the National Council of Teachers of Mathematics standards (NCTM, 1989) emphasized these skills as being on a par with mathematical knowledge.

The chapter ends by describing general rubrics for report writing and creativity that I have developed. These are important school-based skills, and I have noticed that often rubrics for these skills are wanting. For example, "creativity" rubrics are often about artistic presentation rather than true creative accomplishment. I welcome comments, suggestions, and additional examples from readers.

Writing: The 6+1 Trait Writing rubrics

For decades, the 6+1 Trait Writing rubrics have been widely used by teachers, schools, districts, and states. They have become a standard way to look at student writing.

Evidence of effectiveness

A theme of this chapter is that when rubrics clearly characterize what student work should look like, instruction, assessment, and *learning* improve. For the 6+1 Trait Writing rubrics, expert opinion and research bear this out. These rubrics have changed the teaching and learning of writing all across the country.

I asked Judy Arter, a professional developer, author, and researcher who has done extensive work with the 6+1 Trait Writing rubrics, to comment on this notion that clear rubrics help with teaching and learning and that the 6+1 Trait Writing rubrics are perhaps the most widely known example of that. Here is her reply (personal communication, November 21, 2011):

> I agree that 6+1 Traits transformed not only the way we think about writing, but also the way we think about classroom assessment. It certainly changed the way I have viewed assessment. In 1980 people were saying, "We can't assess writing, it's too individualistic." Then it was math problem solving. Now people are saying, "Of course we can assess writing and math problem solving, but we can't assess critical thinking." All it takes is a group of people that try to define, in writing, what good _____ looks like, try it out repeatedly, revise it repeatedly, get examples, etc. The more we do that, especially with learning objectives that are slippery and hard to define, the better off we'll be.

Jan Chappuis, director of the Pearson Assessment Training Institute, says she felt she learned how to teach writing when she went through the Puget Sound Writing Program in the early 1980s. Although she found the writing process transformational for her, there were still problems when it came to conferencing with students and guiding their revisions (personal communication, December 19, 2011). She says:

What I believe the 6+1 Trait rubrics did was take what individual teachers did and put it all together, not just responding to one piece here and one piece there, and put it together to define the domain of writing. It was the first time I'd seen everything I was trying to teach about writing [in one place]. As a guide for teaching, and as a guide for students as they are responding to other students' writing—what do I want feedback on? The 6+1 Trait rubrics really did a wonderful job of filling all those needs, in a way that felt more rigorous, and less idiosyncratic.

Research bears out the experience of Judy Arter, Jan Chappuis, and many teachers, schools, and districts: The 6+1 Trait Writing rubrics clarify the qualities of writing and make it easier to teach and learn. A recent federally funded study (Coe, Hanita, Nishioka, & Smiley, 2011) included 196 teachers and more than 4,000 students in 74 schools in Oregon. The researchers compared posttest essay scores of students of teachers who did and did not have professional development in the 6+1 Trait Writing model. They controlled for students' previous writing performance and school characteristics (poverty level, average hours of writing practice, along with teacher experience in general and in teaching writing) and used a statistical model that acknowledged students were clustered within schools.

This state-of-the-art statistical analysis indicated that using the 6+1 Trait Writing model significantly increased student writing scores, with an estimated effect size of 0.109, a small but stable effect. Students improved significantly in three of the six traits (Organization, Voice, and Word Choice). In the other three traits (Ideas, Sentence Fluency, and Conventions), performance improved but not enough to be statistically significant. This study used more sophisticated research methods than two previous studies of the 6+1 Trait Writing model, one of which found improvement (Arter, Spandel, Culham, & Pollard, 1994) and one of which did not (Kozlow & Bellamy, 2004).

Criteria and levels of performance

The 6+1 Trait Writing rubrics were developed in the 1980s by teachers working with the Northwest Regional Educational Laboratory, now Education Northwest (education-northwest.org). Identifying the six traits was a large part of that work. The six (plus one) traits are the following:

- Ideas
- Organization

- Voice
- Word Choice
- Sentence Fluency
- Conventions
- (Presentation)

The "plus one" criterion, Presentation, is used when presenting a polished, published written product is part of what students are intended to learn.

Originally, the criteria had five performance levels. A more recent version with six performance levels, which also can be divided according to Proficient/Not Proficient, has been developed. Appendix A shows the six-point rubrics for grades 3 through 12. Notice that each element in the performance description is listed in its own lettered row, making it easy to see the parallels in the descriptions across levels and also making it easier for students to see how to engineer improvement on a particular trait in their writing.

Education Northwest has also prepared a version of the six-point 6+1 Trait Writing rubrics for K–2 students. The K–2 version includes examples of student work as part of the performance-level descriptions. Appendix B presents this version of the rubrics.

Writing as a performance domain

If you are not familiar with the 6+1 Trait Writing rubrics, I suggest you read them first and then try to apply them to a set of student work. You will see how nicely these rubrics focus your review of student work on the substance of students' writing and how the students harnessed language to convey that substance.

If your students are not familiar with the 6+1 Trait Writing rubrics, it's a good idea to introduce them one at a time (for example, the rubric for Ideas), using examples of work at each level as well as the rubrics themselves (Arter et al., 1994). Jan Chappuis points out that using the 6+1 Trait Writing rubrics allows teachers of writing to go beyond formulaic teaching of writing and really delve into the heart of it (personal communication, December 19, 2011):

> When they are giving kids 5 points for this and 5 points for that, often the teachers' vision of quality [writing] is not clear enough. This problem is the one the 6 Traits solve so beautifully. . . . The two things going on in. . . Ideas are focus and details. How do I teach kids lessons on what is a narrow focus? No amount of teaching how to write a topic sentence and supporting details

will get you there. When you teach main idea, this is what you're getting at, but a better way is to work on focus and support. . . . Give them tightly focused topics first, teach them how to select details that are interesting and important, give them mini-lessons. . . . What are the main ideas inside each trait, then you teach to those pieces, you ask students to self-assess on those pieces. When a student's piece is an organizational mess, often the problem is focus. I've found the 6 Traits not only good for assessing and teaching . . . but also how to diagnose problems and where to start.

Notice that each of the six traits (seven, if you count Presentation) employs a key question to focus students and teachers on the meaning of the trait, and then four to six elements identifying characteristics to look for in the writing. For clarity, the elements are lettered. The elements are not the traits (or criteria, in the language I have been using in this book). The elements are "look-fors": indicators or pointers toward the criteria.

For example, the key question for the Ideas trait is "Does the writer stay focused and share original and fresh information or perspective on the topic?" The rubric identifies six elements to look for in the writing: (a) a narrow topic, (b) strong support for that topic, (c) relevant details, (d) original ideas based on the author's own experience, (e) readers' questions being answered, and (f) author helping readers make connections with the writing. Each of these elements could support generating examples, targeted instruction, student practice using the writing process, self-assessment, peer assessment, and teacher feedback.

Examples for designing effective rubrics

The 6+1 Trait Writing rubrics, in my opinion, did more than revolutionize the teaching and learning of writing. They showed people what this new tool called "rubrics" could and should do.

The 6+1 Trait Writing rubrics are instructive for designing other kinds of rubrics because they illustrate good ways around the two main pitfalls that are so easy for writers of rubrics to fall into. First, they show how to avoid counting and other formulaic approaches to description. Second, they show how to avoid narrow description that leaves room for only one kind of good answer, and instead allow for multiple routes to quality work. The antidote to both of these pitfalls is to describe what the work should accomplish. The 6+1 Trait Writing rubrics do this by using a key question for each trait and, for each element, describing the effect that successful work has on the reader.

Probably my favorite example of that is how these rubrics show teachers and other educators another way to evaluate grammar besides counting errors. In the Conventions trait, grammar per se is not the issue. Rather, as the key question shows, the issue is how much editing would be needed for readers to be able to understand the meaning the writer is trying to communicate. Even for Exceptional (Level 6) performance, "Author uses standard writing conventions effectively to enhance readability; errors are few and only minor editing is needed to publish." The desired quality is not "zero errors," but rather "readable."

Another favorite example of mine is how the Organization trait allows for multiple routes to quality work. Many elementary teachers instruct their students in paragraph writing with a formulaic approach. Students start with a topic sentence, list three supporting details, and end with a concluding sentence. This is not a bad protocol, but it is also not the only way to write an organized paragraph. Similarly, some high school writing instruction teaches a five-paragraph essay format. Again, this is not a bad protocol, but it is not the only approach. The key question for the Organization trait again is reading for meaning: "Does the organizational structure enhance the ideas and make the piece easier to understand?"

> ### SELF-REFLECTION
>
> Do you use the 6+1 Trait Writing rubrics in your teaching? Did you learn to write using the 6+1 Trait Writing rubrics when you were in school? What has been your experience with them?

Mathematics problem solving

Mathematics teachers seem to agree on the qualities of effective mathematics problem solving. Many mathematics problem-solving rubrics now use three dimensions: Mathematical Conceptual and Procedural Knowledge, Strategic Knowledge, and Mathematical Communication. Although you will still find many different mathematics problem-solving rubrics, almost all of them use these dimensions, sometimes with mathematical conceptual and procedural knowledge appeared as separate criteria. These dimensions are found in rubrics for research, for state test programs, and for the classroom.

Lane, Liu, Ankenmann, and Stone (1996) used rubrics for research on the assessment of mathematical problem solving that were based, in part, on rubrics used for a state testing program at the time (California State Department of Education, 1989). Attributes they considered under each criterion included the following:

- *Mathematical knowledge:* Understanding the problem's mathematical concepts and principles, using mathematical terminology and notation, execution of algorithms, and calculation accuracy.
- *Strategic knowledge:* Use of relevant outside information, identifying elements of the problem and their relationships, use of a solution process, and whether that process is systematic and complete.
- *Mathematical communication:* Completeness of response, clarity of explanations and descriptions, appropriateness of diagrams, communication to audience, and soundness (logic and support) of arguments.

Renee Parker (Parker & Breyfogle, 2011) found the same elements were important in teaching 3rd graders how to solve problems and write about them in ways that would prepare them to do well on the Pennsylvania System of School Assessment (PSSA). Using problems based on released items from the PSSA and a student-friendly rubric she found on the Illinois State Department of Education website, she developed a problem set and associated rubric. Ms. Parker adapted the Illinois rubric to be even more appropriate for 3rd graders. She used nouns instead of pronouns (for example, "the problem" instead of "it"), made sure all verbs were simple and active, and changed some words to match the language of elementary mathematics instruction. Parker and Breyfogle's student-friendly rubric for elementary mathematics problem solving is shown in Figure 4.1. This rubric assessed the same problem-solving elements—mathematics concepts, planning and using strategies, and explaining mathematics work in writing—as did Lane and her colleagues; as did California, Pennsylvania, and Illinois; and, in fact, as do many other schools, districts, and states too numerous to cite here.

Parker and Breyfogle titled their project "Learning to Write About Mathematics." Ms. Parker had embarked on her project because, although her students could solve problems, they had trouble explaining their reasoning. Mathematical communication was the area in which her students needed to improve the most, and, in fact, they did just that. By the end of five weeks, average and below-average students were able to explain their reasoning as well as her above-average students. The rubric itself didn't do the trick. What did it was using the rubric in a series of class activities and individual conferences, helping the students talk about the criteria and how their work and others' work met them.

We'll talk more about how Ms. Parker used the rubric in Chapter 10. The purpose for showing it in this chapter is to analyze its construction. As noted, this rubric is student friendly. It is written from the students' point of view, using first person, in language the students can understand. It is a great example of how "student-friendly language"

Figure 4.1   Math Problem-Solving Rubric

Math Problem-Solving Rubric

Your score	SHOWING MATH KNOWLEDGE (Can you do the problem correctly?)	USING PROBLEM-SOLVING STRATEGIES (How do you solve the problem?)	WRITING AN EXPLANATION (Can you explain your work?)
5	• I figure out the correct answer. • I solve the problem with no mistakes.	• I use all the important information from the problem. • I show all the steps I used to solve the problem. • I make a drawing to show how I solved the problem	• I write **what** I did and **why** I did it. • I explain **each step** of my work. • I use **math words and strategy names**. • I write the **answer in a complete sentence** at the end of my explanation.
4	• I figure out the correct answer. • I solve the problem, but I make a few **small mistakes**.	• I use most of the **important information** from the problem. • I show **most of the steps** I used to solve the problem.	• I write **what** I did and a little about **why** I did it. • I explain **most** of my work.
3	• I figure out part of the answer. • I try to solve the problem, but I make **some big mistakes**.	• I use some of the **important information** from the problem. • I show **some of the steps** I used to solve the problem.	• I write a little about **what** I did or **why** I did it, but not both. • I explain **some** of my work.
2	• I try to solve the problem, but I **don't understand it**.	• I use very little **important information** from the problem. • I show almost none of the steps I used to solve the problem.	• I write something that **doesn't make sense**. • I write an **unclear answer**.
1	• I **don't try** to solve the problem.	• I show no steps that I used to solve the problem.	• I **don't write anything** to explain how I solved the problem.

Source: From "Learning to write about mathematics," by R. Parker and M. L. Breyfogle, 2011, *Teaching Children Mathematics, 18*(2), online appendix. Available http://www.nctm.org/uploadedFiles/Journals_and_Books/TCM/article-2011-Vol18/Extras-2011-Vol18/tcm2011-09-90z1.pdf. Reprinted with permission.

does *not* mean simply easy vocabulary. It means that the descriptions are expressed in the manner that students would think about their work. Thus student-friendly language is not simply a matter of writing style; it's also about students' ways of thinking.

Probably the most important illustration in this rubric of expressing thinking from the students' point of view is in the descriptions of levels of performance for the Showing Math Knowledge criterion. Mathematics problem-solving rubrics written for adults describe students' work in terms like "shows understanding of mathematical concepts and principles," "uses appropriate terms and notations," and "executes algorithms completely and correctly." But you can't ask students to evaluate their own "understanding of mathematical concepts and principles." That is a judgment that must be made by an external observer. In this student-friendly rubric, the concept of understanding has been flipped over, from what the adult would observe to what the student would do. So the language became "I figure out . . . ." Student understanding of mathematical concepts and principles is exhibited in the course of "figuring out" the solution to the problem.

> ### SELF-REFLECTION
>
> If you are an elementary school teacher, how can you envision using the Math Problem-Solving Rubric in your classroom? If you teach secondary school mathematics, how might you adapt this rubric for your students?

The other two criteria, Using Problem-Solving Strategies and Writing an Explanation, similarly use this flipping principle, describing not what an adult would observe but what a student would do. For example, "I use all the important information . . ." is what a student does when an adult would conclude that the student identified all the important elements of a problem. In these two criteria, incorporating how students would think, as well as speak, about their work into student-friendly language is not quite as obvious as for the knowledge criterion, but it's there nonetheless.

Writing reports

Written reports are important assignments in many different subject areas. Typically the teacher's intention is for the students to learn some facts and concepts about the topic, analyze or process the material so that it answers a question or in some way becomes a property of the student and not just a regurgitation of sources, and communicate the results in the format of a term paper or report. That means the content, the thinking, and the report writing are all important criteria. The rubric in Figure 4.2 reflects these criteria.

Figure 4.2   General Rubric for Written Projects (may be adapted for specific projects)

	Content	Reasoning & Evidence	Clarity
4	The thesis is clear A large amount and variety of material and evidence support the thesis. All material is relevant. This material includes details. Information is accurate. Appropriate sources were consulted.	Information is clearly and explicitly related to the point(s) the material is intended to support. Information is organized in a logical manner and is presented concisely. Flow is good. Introductions, transitions, and other connecting material take the listener/reader along.	Few errors of grammar and usage; any minor errors do not interfere with meaning. Language style and word choice are highly effective and enhance meaning. Style and word choice are appropriate to the project.
3	The thesis is clear An adequate amount of material and evidence supports the thesis. Most material is relevant. This material includes details. Information is mostly accurate; any inaccuracies are minor and do not interfere with the points made. Appropriate sources were consulted.	Information is clearly related to the point(s) the material is intended to support, although not all connections may be explained. Information is organized in a logical manner. Flow is adequate. Introductions, transitions, and other connecting material take the listener/reader along for the most part. Any abrupt transitions do not interfere with intended meaning.	Some errors of grammar and usage; errors do not interfere with meaning. Language style and word choice are for the most part effective and appropriate to the project.

continued

Figure 4.2   General Rubric for Written Projects (may be adapted for specific projects) *(continued)*

	Content	Reasoning & Evidence	Clarity
2	The thesis may be somewhat unclear. Some material and evidence support the thesis. Some of the material is relevant, and some is not. Details are lacking. Information may include some inaccuracies. At least some sources were appropriate.	Some of the information is related to the point(s) the material is intended to support, but connections are not explained. Information is not entirely organized in a logical manner, although some structure is apparent. Flow is choppy. Introductions, transitions, and other connecting material may be lacking or unsuccessful.	Major errors of grammar and usage begin to interfere with meaning. Language style and word choce are simple, bland, otherwise not very effective or not entirely appropriate.
1	The thesis is not clear. Much of the material may be irrelevant to the overall topic or inaccurate. Details are lacking. Appropriate sources were not consulted.	Information is not related to the point(s) the material is intended to support. Information is organized in a logical manner. Material does not flow. Information is presented as a sequence of unrelated material.	Major errors of grammar and usage make meaning unclear. Language style and word choice are ineffective and/or inappropriate.

Source: From *How to give effective feedback to your students* (pp. 63–64), by S. M. Brookhart, 2008, Alexandria, VA: ASCD. Copyright 2008 by ASCD. Reprinted with permission.

This rubric also reflects changes in my own thinking about assessing term papers and written reports (Brookhart, 1993). I have been persuaded in my own work with teachers and students, and by advances in the field shown in the work of colleagues (Arter & Chappuis, 2006), that general rubrics, used repeatedly for assessing similar skills, help students learn.

General analytic rubrics that define for students what the criteria are for good report writing as an overall skill, and that focus students on descriptions of quality of work for those criteria, are useful not only for grading but also for learning. As students use these rubrics on several different reports, they learn to focus on the elements of content (Do I have a thesis? Do I support it with detailed, accurate, relevant material? Did I get the material from appropriate sources?), reasoning and evidence (Did I write logically? Is it clear how my details support my main points? Can a reader follow my reasoning?), and clarity (Did I write clearly?).

Strategies for getting students to use rubrics to learn and to monitor their learning are shared in Chapters 9 and 10. Strategies for using rubrics for grading are presented in Chapter 11, although here I would foreshadow that discussion by noting that for some written reports the Content criterion might count double. For now, it is sufficient to see how the descriptions in these rubrics are general and would bear up under repeated use for a fundamental skill such as report writing.

Creativity

Creativity is a general skill that is often incorporated as one of the criteria in task-based rubrics for all sorts of written, oral, and graphic student products. "Wait!" you say. "How can you assess creativity? Isn't creativity some ineffable quality, some inspiration that just springs from the mind in a flash of insight?" Actually, not so. Creative people do have flashes of insight, but their creative processes are not different in kind from "normal" thinking. Creativity is the exceptional use of "familiar mental operations such as remembering, understanding, and recognizing" (Perkins, 1981, p. 274). If we can name the sorts of things that creative students do, we can teach creativity and assess it. And we need to do a better job of that than often happens.

Creativity is sometimes misinterpreted as a description of student work that is visually interesting or persuasive or exciting (Brookhart, 2010). If this is the case, it is much better to call the criterion what it is—visual attractiveness, persuasiveness, or whatever. A pretty cover on a report may be "creative," but it is much more likely to be simply a good use of media (hand lettering and coloring or computer clip art, perhaps), more akin to a visual arts skill than creativity. Once the criterion is appropriately named, it may drop off the list because it becomes clear that it is not really related to the learning outcomes of interest.

I have seen creativity criteria in rubrics that intended to assess originality, and that's closer to the mark. The top category for a Creativity/Originality criterion describes work as very original, creative, inventive, imaginative, unique, and so on. The levels below devolve from that, with work described as using other people's ideas, like everyone else's, not very imaginative, and the like. Such rubrics work for me, and they can work for students and teachers to the degree that they have good examples to show what "original" means. These would be examples not for students to emulate the content, but for them to emulate the way in which the content stands out from others.

However, there is more to creativity than just originality, and as we have seen in the 6+1 Trait Writing rubrics, the more clearly you define the criteria, the more helpful you will be to students. If you ask, "What do creative students do?" the answer can be summarized into four categories. Creative students do the following:

- Recognize the importance of a deep knowledge base and continually work to learn new things.
- Are open to new ideas and actively seek them out.
- Find source material in a wide variety of media, people, and events.
- Organize and reorganize ideas into different categories or combinations and then evaluate whether the results are interesting, new, or helpful.
- Use trial and error if they are not sure how to proceed, viewing failure as opportunity to learn. (Brookhart, 2010, pp. 128–129)

If these are the characteristics of creative students, then these characteristics should be evident in their work. Excluding the last one—which is more of a personal trait than something that would result in evidence in any one specific piece of work—we can derive four criteria for creative work:

- Depth and quality of ideas
- Variety of sources
- Organization and combination of ideas
- Originality of contribution

Figure 4.3 organizes these criteria into an analytic rubric. I have written the descriptions of performance along a continuum that could be labeled *4, 3, 2, 1*, with *3* being the Proficient level. Because "proficient at creativity" doesn't sound right, I have labeled the levels Very Creative, Creative, Ordinary/Routine, and Imitative. Although no one wants to be "imitative," there *are* times when ordinary work is appropriate. For assignments and assessments where this is the case, my advice is don't ask for creative work and don't use a rubric (or any other means) to assess it.

Many major assignments already have analytic rubrics associated with them. In that situation, adding four more rubric scales to the assessment might be a bit much. Figure 4.4 organizes the same four criteria for creativity—Ideas, Sources, Organization/Combination, and Originality—into one holistic rubric for creativity. Note that there are still four criteria; it's just that they are considered simultaneously. So although the rubric in Figure 4.4 looks one-dimensional, it's very different from a creativity scale that lists, for example, "very creative, creative, not creative," or something like that. And although you might use the holistic rubric in Figure 4.4 for grading, the analytic version in Figure 4.3 would be better for teaching and learning.

> **SELF-REFLECTION**
>
> Do you use rubrics for written reports or for creativity in your teaching? What has been your experience with them? How does that experience help you interpret the information about rubrics for written reports and for creativity in this chapter?

Summing up

This chapter had two main purposes. The first was to make the case for using general, analytic rubrics for fundamental skills. General, analytic rubrics that are worth students' time and effort are the antithesis of the task-based, "directions"-style rubrics that count things rather than evaluate quality. General, analytic rubrics are good for learning as well as for grading.

The second purpose was to show several wonderful examples. Each of them illustrates the two defining characteristics of rubrics: appropriate criteria and, for each criterion, descriptions of performance along a continuum of quality. Their use of language and their treatment of both the criteria and performance-level descriptions will help you as you prepare your own criteria and performance-level descriptions. Most important,

Figure 4.3   Analytic Rubric for Creativity

	Very Creative	Creative	Ordinary/Routine	Imitative
Depth and Quality of Ideas	Ideas represent a startling variety of important concepts from different contexts or disciplines.	Ideas represent important concepts from different contexts or disciplines.	Ideas represent important concepts from the same or similar contexts or disciplines.	Ideas do not represent important concepts.
Variety of Sources	Created product draws on a wide-ranging variety of sources, including different texts, media, resource persons, and/or personal experiences.	Created product draws on a variety of sources, including different texts, media, resource persons, and/or personal experiences.	Created product draws on a limited set of sources and media.	Created product draws on only one source, and/or sources are not trustworthy or appropriate.
Organization and Combination of Ideas	Ideas are combined in original and surprising ways to solve a problem, address an issue, or make something new.	Ideas are combined in original ways to solve a problem, address an issue, or make something new.	Ideas are combined in ways that are derived from the thinking of others (for example, of the authors in sources consulted).	Ideas are copied or restated from the source(s) consulted.
Originality of Contribution	Created product is interesting, new, and/or helpful, making an original contribution that includes identifying a previously unknown problem, issue, or purpose.	Created product is interesting, new, and/or helpful, making an original contribution for its intended purpose (e.g., solving a problem or addressing an issue).	Created product serves its intended purpose (e.g., solving a problem or addressing an issue).	Created product does not serve its intended purpose (e.g., solving a problem or addressing an issue).

Figure 4.4   **Holistic Rubric for Creativity**

Very Creative	Ideas represent a startling variety of important concepts from different contexts or disciplines. Created product draws on a wide-ranging variety of sources, including different texts, media, resource persons, and/or personal experiences. Ideas are combined in original and surprising ways to solve a problem, address an issue, or make something new. Created product is interesting, new, and/or helpful, making an original contribution that includes identifying a previously unknown problem, issue, or purpose.
Creative	Ideas represent important concepts from different contexts or disciplines. Created product draws on a variety of sources, including different texts, media, resource persons, and/or personal experiences. Ideas are combined in original ways to solve a problem, address an issue, or make something new. Created product is interesting, new, and/or helpful, making an original contribution for its intended purpose (e.g., solving a problem or addressing an issue).
Ordinary/Routine	Ideas represent important concepts from the same or similar contexts or disciplines. Created product draws on a limited set of sources and media. Ideas are combined in ways that are derived from the thinking of others (e.g., of the authors in sources consulted). Created product serves its intended purpose (e.g., solving a problem or addressing an issue).
Imitative	Ideas do not represent important concepts. Created product draws on only one source, and/or sources are not trustworthy or appropriate. Ideas are copied or restated from the source(s) consulted. Created product does not serve its intended purpose (e.g., solving a problem or addressing an issue).

the way the rubrics in this chapter use criteria and performance-level descriptions should help you get a better sense of the nature of those two defining characteristics of rubrics, another main theme of the book.

There are some occasions when task-specific rubrics are useful. The next chapter considers task-specific rubrics and how to use them.

5

Task-Specific Rubrics and Scoring Schemes for Special Purposes

For me and for others who work with teachers and rubrics (Arter & Chappuis, 2006; Arter & McTighe, 2001; Chappuis, 2009), the advantages that come with using rubrics to support student learning are so significant that we more or less recommend you always use general rubrics, except in special cases. In this chapter we explore those special cases. Don't be fooled, however, into thinking that means you should use task-specific rubrics if general rubrics are more appropriate.

When to use task-specific rubrics

The special purposes for which task-specific rubrics are useful are related to grading. In particular, task-specific rubrics are useful for grading student work intended to assess recall and comprehension of a body of knowledge—remembering and understanding facts and concepts.

Task-specific rubrics are easier than general rubrics to use reliably without a lot of practice. It requires less inference to match a description of a right answer than to make a more abstract judgment to match a description of performance quality. There are a few grading purposes that capitalize on this one positive feature of task-specific rubrics. When you are grading test questions for a final exam or any kind of test where students will see only their grade and have no opportunity for feedback, revision, or further learning, task-specific rubrics for individual test questions make for quick, reliable grading. Figure 5.1 gives an example of a task-specific rubric for a 4th grade mathematics problem that requires students to solve a multistep problem and explain their reasoning.

Figure 5.1   **A Mathematics Problem Scored with a Task-Specific Rubric**

The Problem

AMUSEMENT PARK
70 things to do!
34 rides
plus games
plus shows

An amusement park has games, rides, and shows.

- The total number of games, rides, and shows is 70.
- There are 34 rides.
- There are two times as many games as shows.

How many games are there? _____

How many shows are there? _____

Use numbers, words, or drawings to show how you got your answer.

If you need more room for your work, use the space below.

Task-Specific Scoring Rubric

Extended
24 games and 12 shows with correct explanation or work

Sample Correct Response:
70−34=36 so there are 36 shows and games.
The number of games is twice the number of shows; there must be 24 games and 12 shows.

continued

Figure 5.1   A Mathematics Problem Scored with a Task-Specific Rubric (*continued*)

Satisfactory
Has subtraction error but has games and shows in correct ratio (2:1)
OR
Has 12 games and 24 shows with work
OR
Has 24 games and 12 shows with no work

Partial
Finds 36, and has ratio of 2 to 1 (but not 24 to 12) and sum of games and shows is less than 36
OR
Has 36 games and 18 shows with or without work
OR
Has 72 games and 36 shows with or without work
OR
Shows a process that reflects understanding of the question, but does not find the correct ratio

Minimal
Finds 36 by subtraction or adding on to 34 to get 70
OR
Number of games plus number of shows is 36
OR
Has games and shows in a two to one ratio but nothing else correct

Incorrect
Incorrect response

Source: National Assessment of Educational Progress released items: 2011, grade 4, block M8, question #19. Available: http://nces.ed.gov/nationsreportcard/itmrlsx/

Grading essay or other multipoint test questions with task-specific rubrics

Task-specific scoring guides can be true rubrics, with criteria and descriptions of performance at each level of quality. The example in Figure 5.1 shows how task-specific rubrics would be useful for scoring a constructed-response test item in which students have to solve a problem and then explain their reasoning. In this case, there are five score levels. You could use task-specific rubrics with any number of levels of multipoint scoring. Once you get beyond right/wrong (1/0) scoring, you need some sort of scoring scheme to allocate the points. Even a simple Completely Correct/Partially Correct/

Incorrect (2-1-0 or 3-2-1) scoring scheme needs descriptive information so you know how to decide what level a student's response exemplifies.

Brief essay questions on tests often use multipoint scoring as well. Figure 5.2 presents an example of an essay question and a task-specific rubric a teacher would use to score it.

Figure 5.2   A Science Essay Test Question Scored with a Task-Specific Rubric

Question
Lightning and thunder happen at the same time, but you see the lightning before you hear the thunder. Explain why this is so.

Task-Specific Scoring Rubric

Complete
Student responds that although the thunder and lightning occur at the same time, light travels faster than sound so the light gets to your eye before the sound reaches your ear.

Partial
Student response addresses speed and uses terminology such as thunder for sound and lightning for light, or makes a general statement about speed but does not tell which is faster.

Unsatisfactory/Incorrect
Student response does not relate the speeds at which light and sound travel.

Source: National Assessment of Educational Progress released items: 2005, grade 4, block S13, question #10. Available: http://nces.ed.gov/nationsreportcard/itmrlsx/

As you look at the examples in Figures 5.1 and 5.2, you are probably noticing an important point—namely, that they are holistic (as opposed to analytic) rubrics. The criteria for good work are all considered together. In the mathematics problem-solving example, identifying the operations required for the problem, selecting and using the right numbers, calculating correctly, and communicating the explanation by showing all work are all assessed at once. In the science essay example, identifying the issue as one of relative speed of travel and communicating that clearly are assessed together. This approach is appropriate for questions on a test, where the score for individual questions will be combined with scores for other questions to make a total test score. The advantage of analytic rubrics, which allow students to receive feedback on the criteria individually and use it for improvement, makes little difference in this case.

Writing task-specific rubrics

Writing task-specific rubrics for multipoint test questions differs from writing general rubrics for you and students to use together for both formative and summative assessment. The first and most obvious difference is that for task-specific rubrics, you write directly for a task. Remember that for general rubrics, you don't write directly for a task. Instead, you use criteria that describe the learning that would be demonstrated in any one of a whole class of tasks.

Second, writing task-specific rubrics differs from writing general rubrics because you can use teacher language. Students do not use task-specific rubrics. Therefore, you can use adult vocabulary, bulleted lists, sample answers, and any combination of notes that makes clear to you what you should be looking for at each level of performance. One thing to be careful of, however, is to leave room for multiple good answers if the questions have multiple good answers. For example, sometimes there are several ways to explain mathematical reasoning. Some essay questions ask students to draw a conclusion and support it, and there might be several tenable answers. Make sure your task-specific rubrics give appropriate points to all answers that merit them, not just to the answer that you would have written if you were the student.

Third, you write task-specific rubrics at the same time that you write the test question. Typically you will have a test blueprint and will know how many points are required. Therefore, the decision about the number of performance levels is usually more or less made for you. Solve the problem or write an answer that is complete and correct and, in your view, would deserve full points. Describe that answer and then write descriptions of answers that would qualify for fewer and fewer points, until you get to "no answer" or "totally incorrect answer" or something like that for the lowest point value. In most cases, the lowest point value for a task-specific rubric for a classroom test question will be zero, consistent with the questions scored right/wrong (where a wrong answer is worth zero points).

Grading essay or other multipoint test questions with point-based scoring schemes

Sometimes essay test questions or other multipoint test questions are used to assess whether students can recall a concept and explain it in their own words. Other multipoint test questions can assess student understanding of a body of knowledge; for example, a question might ask students to list and explain steps in a scientific process.

I hope these are not the only, or even the main, type of constructed-response test questions you pose for your students (Brookhart, 2010). However, for questions like this, a point-based scoring scheme works well—often better than task-specific rubrics would. There are at least two reasons this is so. One, in a point-based scoring scheme, points can be allocated to the various facts and concepts in the body of knowledge you intend to assess in a manner that weights knowledge of the various elements according to their importance. Two, a point-based scoring scheme enumerates the elements—the facts and concepts. Thus if recalling specific information is what the question intends to assess, this enumeration allows you to check for each one. Figure 5.3 shows an example of a point-based scoring scheme for an elementary social studies test question.

Figure 5.3   A Social Studies Test Question Scored with a Point Scheme

Question
Fill in the chart below with the name of each of the three branches of government and the main purpose of each branch.

Branch of Government	Main Purpose

Point-Based Scoring Rubric
Total possible points = 6
1 point each for naming the executive, legislative, and judicial branches
1 point each for listing the main purpose, at minimum:

- Executive branch—Enforces laws
- Legislative branch—Makes laws
- Judicial branch—Interprets laws

Writing point-based scoring schemes

To write point-based scoring schemes, identify the major facts and concepts and any other elements of the body of knowledge you are trying to assess. List them.

Look at the elements in your list and decide whether they all contribute to the answer in the same proportion—that is, with the same weight—or if some elements (facts, concepts, explanations, and so on) are more important than others. Allocate points accordingly. If the point-based scoring scheme is for one question on a test, make sure that the number of points for the question gives it the weight it should contribute to the total test score. If not, adjust either the question or the point scheme until it does.

In some cases, your point-based scoring scheme will specify that each fact, concept, explanation, or other element of the body of knowledge you are testing must be present in the students' answers. The example in Figure 5.3 uses this kind of point-based scoring scheme.

In other cases, you might specify the points that will be earned for up to some number of a larger number of possible elements. For example, say you have just taught a unit on the causes of the Civil War. Therefore, an essay question asking students to identify and briefly explain causes of the Civil War would require recall and comprehension. A point-based scoring scheme might say students would receive one point each for identifying up to four from a longer list of possible causes, and one point each for correct explanations, up to a possible eight points for the question. Notice that this differs from effective performance-level descriptions in rubrics, where counting things is discouraged except in special cases. This kind of "counting" can work in point-based scoring schemes for questions that are about recall of facts and concepts, because enumerating facts and concepts is precisely what you are trying to assess.

> **SELF-REFLECTION**
>
> Can you envision a use for task-specific rubrics or point-based scoring schemes in your classroom? How does this use fit with the discussion of task-specific rubrics and point-based scoring schemes in this chapter?

Summing up

Task-specific rubrics serve a purpose—namely, grading. A book about rubrics wouldn't be complete without discussing task-specific rubrics, and that has been the purpose of this chapter. This chapter also considered point-based scoring schemes that are not rubrics, again for the sake of completeness. Task-specific rubrics and point-based scoring schemes are two methods you should have in your scoring repertoire, even if they aren't the most important ones.

General rubrics are much more flexible and serve at least two purposes: learning and grading. And general rubrics can be used with students, which is why I consider them more important than task-specific rubrics. A special case of using general rubrics occurs when schools and teachers adopt standards-based grading policies based on demonstrating proficiency levels and coordinate all their rubrics. This situation requires consensus from all the teachers in a grade or department that teach the same standards. If the consensus exists, however, then assessment is simplified in some ways. Chapter 6 discusses proficiency-based rubrics that assist in standards-based grading.

6

Proficiency-Based Rubrics
for Standards-Based Grading

Proficiency-based rubrics are rubrics aligned with standards-based grading scales from the start, so that progress is described in terms of achievement of that standard. Proficiency-based rubrics use the same scale—the same levels of achievement—for each assessment, including both tests and performance assessments. Therefore, proficiency-based rubrics document student performance in terms of proficiency level on a standard.

Although this might sound like simply using special rubrics—and in practice that's what happens—consistent use of proficiency-based rubrics for all assessments changes the point of reference for interpreting student performance. It's actually more of a shift than it looks like.

SELF-REFLECTION

Does your school use standards-based grading? Have you noticed any advantages of standards-based grading compared with traditional grading? If you do use standards-based grading, do you use the same proficiency scale for each assessment on a standard?

Think about the traditional number-right and percentage scales used to grade many tests. The base of that percentage is a number that represents the test content, not the standard directly. Suppose a student scores 100 percent on a test. If you use standards-based grading, you might be tempted to say that student is "Advanced." But what if that test measured only the basic comprehension required for the standard and did not ask any questions whose answers required advanced thinking? That 100 percent really indicates that the student is "Proficient." You would need a different assessment, one that has questions or tasks that would allow advanced students to demonstrate extended thinking, to know whether students could do that.

How to create proficiency-based rubrics

You can create proficiency-based rubrics in three steps. First, design a general framework based on the number and names of proficiency levels, and what they are intended to mean, in your school or district. Second, write general rubrics for each standard, based on the framework. Third, for each assessment on that standard, describe the specific performance requirements for each level.

Create the general framework

Proficiency-based rubrics begin with general rubrics that describe the expectations for each level of proficiency, in the same terms as your standards-based report card. For some districts, the levels are the same as for their state proficiency tests, but this is not necessarily the case.

Identify the number and names of proficiency levels. Most educators know this already, but it is worth mentioning as the first step because it is the foundation for constructing proficiency-based rubrics. If your standards-based report cards use four levels, titled Advanced, Proficient, Nearing Proficient, and Novice, then those are the levels to use. If your standards-based report cards use some other levels, use those.

Describe what each level means in your system. Sometimes proficiency levels are described in generic terms on standards-based report cards and their supporting documents. Sometimes report cards have definitions, but they are not really helpful descriptions to use as the basis for rubrics. For example, they may simply repeat the level name (for example, "Performs at an advanced level" and so on). If useful general descriptions of what performance at each level means already exist, use them.

If such descriptions do not already exist, you need to design them. Use a team of teachers to do this. The question of "how proficient a student needs to be to be proficient" should be decided collegially and not by any one administrator or teacher. Figure 6.1 presents an example of a general framework for proficiency-based rubrics using four levels of proficiency.

Figure 6.1   Sample General Framework for Proficiency-Based Rubrics

4 **Advanced**	Shows a thorough understanding of the concept or skill, and extends understanding beyond the requirements of the standard (e.g., by relating concept to other concepts, by offering new ideas, by a deep and nuanced analysis, or by demonstrating a level of skill beyond expectations for proficiency).
3 **Proficient**	Shows a complete and correct understanding of the concept or the ability to perform the skill as articulated in the standard.
2 **Nearing Proficient**	Shows partial mastery of prerequisite knowledge and a rudimentary or incomplete understanding of the concept or a rudimentary ability to perform the skill as articulated in the standard.
1 **Novice**	Shows serious misconceptions or lack of understanding of the concept or an inability to perform the skill as articulated in the standard.

The example in Figure 6.1 is too general to use as is and is not meant to be used for formative assessment or grading. It is a general framework or template for your thinking as you make more specific rubrics for individual assignments.

Write a general rubric for each standard

For each standard you are going to assess, adapt the general framework into a general rubric for the standard. If you use standards-based report cards, the "standards" in question will be the reporting standards, which may be a bit more specific than your state standards. If you do not use standards-based report cards, the "standards" in question may be state standards or curricular goals. If your school or district has done curriculum mapping, typically you will use the standards or goals listed on the curriculum map. Figure 6.2 shows a general rubric for the standard "Understands the concept of

Figure 6.2   Rubric for a Specific Standard

Standard: Understands the concept of area and relates area to multiplication and to addition.	
4 **Advanced**	Shows a thorough understanding of the concept of area and the ability to relate this concept to multiplication and addition, and extends understanding by relating area to other concepts or by offering new ideas or by solving extended problems.
3 **Proficient**	Shows a complete and correct understanding of the concept of area and the ability to relate this concept to multiplication and addition.
2 **Nearing Proficient**	Shows partial mastery of prerequisite knowledge (e.g., what plane figures are, how to measure length) and a rudimentary or incomplete understanding of the concept of area.
1 **Novice**	Shows serious misconceptions or lack of understanding of the concept of area.

area and relates area to multiplication and to addition" (CCSSI Standards for Mathematics 3.MD) based on the general framework in Figure 6.1.

One important thing to notice is that the general rubric describes performance in terms that are still too general to use for any particular assessment. The general rubric begs a question at each level—for example, at the Proficient level: What does it look like when a student shows a complete and correct understanding of the concept of area and the ability to relate this concept to multiplication and addition? This is what you will work out for each assessment.

Describe the specific performance requirements

For each assessment on a standard, describe the specific performance requirements for each level. Suppose that a 3rd grade teacher is preparing a mathematics unit and one of the standards she will cover is "Understands the concept of area and relates area to multiplication and to addition." A number of assessments are possible, and although she wouldn't use all of them, she would probably use more than one. Here are some examples of tasks students could do, on a test or performance assessment, to demonstrate comprehension of the concept of area:

- Define or explain what area is, in their own words.
- Distinguish problems that require finding area from those that do not.
- Measure areas by counting unit squares (square centimeters, square meters, square inches, square feet, and square invented units).
- Demonstrate that the area of a rectangle as found by counting square units is the same as the area found by multiplying length and width, and explain their reasoning.
- Use a formula ($A = l \times w$) to find the area of a rectangle.
- Use diagrams to find the area of rectilinear figures by decomposing them into non-overlapping rectangles, and explain their reasoning.
- Construct a model room with rectangular surfaces (floor, walls, windows, sofa and chair seats and backs, etc.), labeling each rectangular surface with its area.
- Write original mathematics problems whose solutions require finding the area; solve the problem and explain reasoning.
- Write real-life problem scenarios whose solutions require finding area; solve the problem and explain reasoning.

Note that these are not fully designed assessments. The list is intended to show that many different assessments could be indicators of the standard.

Notice also that some of these assessments would not provide evidence of Advanced-level understanding because such understanding entails the following: "Shows a thorough understanding of the concept of area and the ability to relate this concept to multiplication and addition, and extends understanding by relating area to other concepts or by offering new ideas or by solving extended problems." Other assessments do allow students, if they are able, to give evidence of extending their understanding.

Consider an assessment in which students are asked to explain what area is, using their own words. The teacher might ask students to do this using a short, constructed-response test item or a stand-alone quiz or oral questioning. In any case, she might use the following specific proficiency-based rubric:

Proficient (3)	Complete and correct explanation.
Nearing Proficient (2)	Partially complete and correct explanation, either missing an important detail or including a small incorrect detail.
Novice (1)	Incorrect explanation, or no explanation.

There is no Advanced (4) level because stating the explanation in your own words does not match the performance expectations for Advanced. The description of Proficient performance matches the description of Proficient in the general rubrics. The teacher would need additional assessments to give evidence of Advanced performance (extending understanding by relating area to other concepts or by offering new ideas or by solving extended problems).

This specific proficiency-based rubric, then, describes what performance at each level looks like on the specific assessment. It is still a general rubric, as opposed to a task-specific rubric, because performance is described in general enough terms that you can share the rubric with students. (A task-specific version of the rubric would include the explanation of area itself, and that is *not* what is needed here.)

Suppose further that the teacher also designs a performance assessment in which she asks students to write a real-life problem scenario whose solution requires finding area, and then to solve the problem and explain their reasoning. (The performance assessment would need more complete directions than that. I don't mean to imply that one sentence alone would suffice for the assignment to students. Because here we are just concerned with the proficiency-based rubrics, we can proceed without that; but it's important enough that I want to clarify and make sure I don't imply that one sentence constitutes a complete assessment.) The teacher might use the following specific proficiency-based rubric:

Advanced (4)	Problem scenario, solution, and explanation show an extended understanding of the concept of area and relate area to multiplication and addition in a detailed analysis, using mathematical language, of an elegant problem solution.
Proficient (3)	Problem scenario, solution, and explanation show a complete and correct understanding of the concept of area and the ability to relate this concept to multiplication and addition.
Nearing Proficient (2)	Problem scenario, solution, and explanation include some flaws and show a rudimentary or incomplete understanding of the concept of area. Relation of area to multiplication and addition is unclear.
Novice (1)	Problem scenario, solution, and explanation show serious misconceptions or a lack of understanding of the concept of area. Relation of area to multiplication and addition is incorrect or not addressed.

Notice that, like the rubric for explaining area in their own words, this rubric is general enough that it may be shared with students at the time the assignment is made. This rubric lends itself to looking at exemplars, supporting student self- and peer assessment, and focusing teacher feedback on work in progress. And an important point is that this specific proficiency-based rubric matches the general proficiency-based rubric for the standard shown in Figure 6.2. A good way to think about it is that each proficiency-based rubric is an instance or special case of the general one.

You can also use proficiency-based rubrics for describing performance on a unit test. Sometimes—but not usually—you can simply define a percentage range for each of the proficiency-based levels described by the general rubric for the standard. I say "not usually" because you can only do that meaningfully when the test covers that standard and no other, and when all the questions are all answerable at all levels, including

Advanced. This is not usually the case. Most tests cover more than one standard or include questions that do not allow Advanced performance.

Suppose the teacher had designed a unit test that included a set of proficiency-level questions about area and its relationship to multiplication and addition, and an open-ended question that allowed students to show extended insights and connections about the concept of area (or not, depending on how the student answered). The teacher might use the following specific proficiency-based rubric:

Advanced (4)	At least 90% correct on proficiency-level questions and a response to the open-ended question that makes connections among area, multiplication, addition, and other concepts.
Proficient (3)	At least 80% correct on proficiency-level questions and a response to the open-ended question that shows comprehension of area and its relation to multiplication and addition.
Nearing Proficient (2)	At least 60% correct on proficiency-level questions and a response to the open-ended question that shows partial understanding of area and its relation to multiplication and addition.
Novice (1)	Less than 60% correct on proficiency-level questions and a response to the open-ended question that shows major misconceptions, or no response to the open-ended question.

Notice that for proficiency-based rubrics, the percentage correct for the total test may not be the appropriate percentage to use. Proficiency-based rubrics require considering the question "percentage of what?" The test might have included questions about other standards as well, and those would not figure in to the assessment of student proficiency on this standard.

How to use proficiency-based rubrics in formative assessment

Use proficiency-based rubrics in all of the same ways you would use any rubrics for formative assessment. Chapters 9 and 10 contain lots of strategies for using rubrics to share learning targets and criteria with students and for using rubrics to help students monitor and regulate their own learning.

It is worth pointing out that proficiency-based rubrics are particularly well suited for a couple of those strategies because the rubrics apply the same meaning about proficiency to all assignments. The two strategies most enhanced by using proficiency-based rubrics are student tracking of their own work and student goal setting.

Student tracking of their own work

The previous section showed that general proficiency-based rubrics for a standard define a general framework for achievement. Each specific assessment and its associated proficiency-based rubric aim to place student achievement within that framework. Therefore, students can track their own work in a meaningful way by recording their proficiency level for each assessment of that standard. The result will be a chart or graph depicting student progress on that standard in the proficiency metric. Figure 6.3 presents an example of a student tracking her achievement on a series of assessments of the standard "Describe the overall structure of a story, including describing how the beginning introduces the story and the ending concludes the action" (CCSS ELA RL 2.5).

Notice that the standard is written in student-friendly language. The student herself records the information and makes the graph. By keeping track of her progress, the student is able to self-reflect, ask questions, develop confidence with the standard, and self-regulate her learning.

Student goal setting

One of the main ways that student goal setting fails is that, in an evaluation-centered classroom culture, students are tempted to express their goals in terms of grades. For example, a student might say, "I want to get an *A* on my next test." More useful student goals are expressed in terms of what students want to learn and how they will know when they have done so—for example, "I want to learn how to retell a story in my own words well enough that my little brother will enjoy listening."

Figure 6.3   Example of a Student Tracking Progress Using Proficiency-Based Rubrics

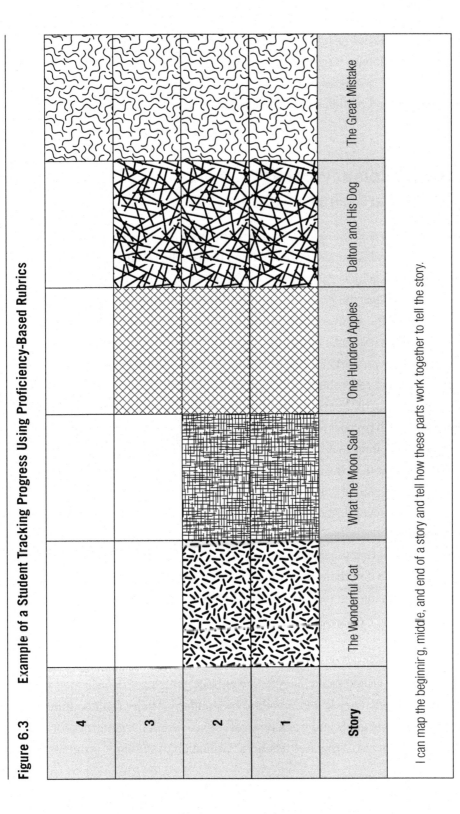

Story	The Wonderful Cat	What the Moon Said	One Hundred Apples	Dalton and His Dog	The Great Mistake
1	▨	▨	▨	▨	▨
2	▨	▨	▨	▨	▨
3				▨	▨
4					▨

I can map the beginning, middle, and end of a story and tell how these parts work together to tell the story.

Proficiency-based rubrics describe performance and therefore are particularly well suited to helping students set goals that describe learning. For example, instead of saying "I want to get a *4*," a student can say, "I want to be able to go beyond the information about the water cycle I read in my textbook and see how I can connect it to the daily weather in my town."

How to use proficiency-based rubrics in standards-based grading

When all of your assessment results for a report period are on the same scale, with the levels having comparable meanings, combining the results is much easier. Look at the pattern of a student's achievement over time for the standard you are evaluating. If the pattern resembles a "learning curve"—starting low, increasing, and then leveling off—take the median of the student's scores for the leveling-off period. These are the scores that represent the student's current achievement with respect to that standard. Figure 6.4 illustrates this scenario for two students, Andrew and Bailey.

If the pattern does not resemble a learning curve, but rather fluctuates up or down over time, take the median of the whole set of scores. This will represent the student's current achievement with respect to that standard as well; unfortunately, in this case it represents a current standing that hasn't improved during the report period. Figure 6.4 also illustrates this scenario, in the example of Cort.

Depending on the design of your report card, you may need to combine final proficiency evaluations from several standards into one grade for a subject or a larger reporting standard. Chapter 11 describes grading procedures in more detail. The purpose of this section is to point out that the special nature of proficiency-based rubrics keyed to standards—all based on a common framework describing proficiency—simplifies final judgments into summarizing a series of comparably rated performances.

Summing up

This chapter has described proficiency-based rubrics, which are coordinated with definitions of various proficiency levels, standard by standard. Their common framework allows students to set goals and track progress. The common framework for proficiency-based rubrics also simplifies teachers' evaluation of students' progress and achievement.

Figure 6.4   Examples of Arriving at a Final Proficiency Grade on One Standard

Student	Standard #1						Standard #2						Summary		
	9/9	9/14	9/22	9/27	10/3	10/6	9/8	9/14	9/21	9/26	10/3	10/7	Std. 1	Std. 2	Std. 3
Andrew	2	1	2	3	3	3							3		
Bailey	2	2	4	3	4	4							4		
Cort	3	1	3	2	3	1							2		
(etc.)															

Add sections for standards and assessments as needed.

Andrew: Andrew's performance on Standard 1 shows the pattern of a learning curve, with a beginning practice period followed by a leveling off of achievement. After beginning at the level of Nearing Proficiency, Andrew's performance on Standard 1 leveled out at a reliable 3, or Proficient, level. The median of his performance after this leveling out is a 3 (median of 3, 3, and 3 = 3).

Bailey: Bailey's performance on Standard 1 shows the pattern of a learning curve. After beginning at the level of Nearing Proficiency, Bailey's performance on Standard 1 leveled out at around 4, or Advanced. The median of her performance after this leveling out is a 4 (median of 4, 3, 4, and 4 = 4).

Cort: Cort's performance does not form the pattern of a learning curve, with a beginning practice period followed by a leveling off of achievement. There is no discernible improvement or decline in his performance on Standard 1 over time. The teacher should try to find out why this is the case. Unless the teacher's investigation finds some reason to revise the proficiency ratings over time, the best summary of Cort's performance is the median of what he has demonstrated, which is a 2, or the Nearing Proficiency level (median of 3, 1, 3, 2, 3, 1 = 2).

7

Checklists and Rating Scales: Not Rubrics, but in the Family

This chapter has two goals. First, I want to distinguish checklists and rating scales from rubrics, with which they are often confused. Don't use checklists and rating scales in situations when rubrics are more appropriate. Second, I want to describe some situations when checklists and rating scales can be useful.

Sometimes people use the term *rubric*—incorrectly—to mean any list-like evaluation tool, and therefore checklists and rating scales are sometimes confused with rubrics. The most important difference between checklists and rating scales on the one hand and rubrics on the other is that checklists and rating scales lack descriptions of performance quality. As we have seen, rubrics are defined by two characteristics: criteria for students' work and descriptions of performance levels. Because checklists and rating scales lack one of these two pieces, they are not rubrics.

Checklists and rating scales do have criteria. The criteria are the "list" of things that you check or rate. Checklists and rating scales are great when you don't need descriptions of performance quality, but rather just need to know whether something has been done (checklist) or how often or how well it has been done (rating scale).

SELF-REFLECTION

Do you use checklists or rating scales in your teaching? For what purposes do you use them? How do you involve students in their use?

Checklists

A checklist is a list of specific characteristics with a place for marking whether that characteristic is present or absent. Checklists by definition break an assignment down into discrete bits (the "list"). This clarifies what is required for the assignment—namely, to do this list of things. Most checklists are easier to use than rubrics because they require low-inference decisions—is something there or isn't it?

Checklists are particularly useful in two kinds of situations. First, checklists are great for both teachers and students to use for situations in which the learning outcomes are defined by the *existence* of an attribute, not its quality. Some simple learning outcomes are like this. For example, many elementary teachers I have worked with use some version of a student checklist for sentencing skills like the example in Figure 7.1. Putting a period at the end of a sentence is a yes-or-no outcome; either the period is there or it isn't. Checklists for writing can be simpler—for example, for kindergarten students the list might include just capital letter, period, and complete idea. Or they can be more complicated, such as including in a checklist for older students the elements of spelling, grammar and usage, and so on.

Figure 7.1   **Sentence Skills Checklist**

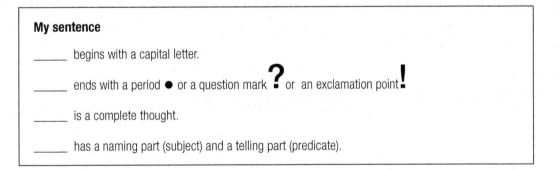

Second, checklists are helpful for students to use to make sure they have followed directions for an assignment, that they have all the required parts of some project, or that they have followed format requirements for a report. Wiliam (2011) calls these "preflight checklists" (p. 141) if they are used before work is turned in. He recommends a technique in which a partner uses the checklist to ascertain an assignment is ready to turn in and becomes accountable for the completeness of the partner's work.

Notice that in this second use the checklist is not the evaluation of the quality of the project. The checklist is used to make sure directions have been followed and all required elements are present. These elements are what get "checked." The teacher will use rubrics based on the criteria for good work—which usually will not be the same as the assignment's required elements. For example, a report checklist might include entries like "Has an introduction," "Has a thesis sentence or research question," "Has at least three sources," "Includes a chart or diagram," and so on, essentially listing the elements required by the directions for the report. The rubrics the teacher and students use to evaluate the quality of the report would include criteria for the understanding and analysis of the topic of the report, clear communication of reasoning and supporting evidence, and so on.

Rating scales

A rating scale is a list of specific characteristics with a place for marking the degree to which each characteristic is displayed. I think of rating scales as two-dimensional check-lists. Like checklists, they break down assignments into discrete bits. However, instead of a yes-no or present-absent decision, rating scales use either frequency or quality ratings —hence the name "rating scale."

Frequency ratings are, unsurprisingly, scales that list the frequency with which some characteristic is observed, from always (or very often) to never (or very seldom), or something like that. They are great to use when you want to serve a purpose similar to that of a checklist—evaluating whether various attributes exist in some work—but the decision is not an all-or-nothing one. Frequency scales are excellent for assessing performance skills (for example, in public speaking, "Makes eye contact" frequently, occasionally, seldom, or never). Frequency scales are also excellent for assessing behaviors, work habits, and other learning skills. Many behaviors are well described by noting whether they occur always, frequently, sometimes, or never, for example.

Figure 7.2 lists several different kinds of frequency scales. To create a rating scale, list the characteristics you wish to assess, as you would for a checklist, and then select the frequency scale that best matches these characteristics. Show the frequency scale as multiple-choice options, as boxes in a table, or as points on a line.

Figure 7.3 shows a frequency scale a high school chemistry teacher used to assist her students in checking their work on volume and temperature problems. The list includes six skills the students needed to use in their work. The frequency scale

Figure 7.2   Examples of Frequency Scales

Scale	Typical Uses
Always, frequently, sometimes, never Consistently, often, sometimes, rarely Always, usually, sometimes, never Almost always, usually, often, occasionally, almost never Very frequently, frequently, occasionally, rarely, very rarely, never *[Four choices are usually sufficient. As illustrated, other numbers of options can be used.]*	To rate how often students exhibit behaviors or learning skills (e.g., works independently; follows directions; completes homework) To rate how often students have certain feelings or attitudes about their work (e.g., I am confident in my work)
All, most, some, none *[Sometimes used with a noun—for example, all problems, most problems, some problems, none of the problems; all sentences, most sentences, some sentences, none of the sentences.]*	To rate how often problems or exercises exhibit certain characteristics (e.g., labeled the answer; showed all work) To rate how often a certain kind of work exhibits desired characteristics (e.g., instead of a checklist for each sentence, students might make an overall rating: My sentences . . . begin with capital letters, have proper punctuation, and so on)

indicates on how many problems (all, most, some, or none) the skill was demonstrated. The student in this example could easily see he should recheck his problems, especially to make sure he had written the Charles's Law equation.

Quality ratings are scales that list judgments of quality—for example, excellent, good, fair, poor. A big problem with quality rating scales is that they are often mistaken for rubrics and used in place of rubrics. Quality ratings are *almost never* helpful for learning. There are at least three reasons for this.

One, quality ratings constitute a rush to judgment in that they skip a step: they pronounce the verdict without describing the evidence. Quality ratings, in effect, declare, "This is excellent because I rated it excellent," and so on. There are "performance levels," but they are not descriptions. I have seen many examples of what were titled

Figure 7.3   A Rating Scale Used for Student Self-Assessment

Skill	On this assignment, I successfully used the skill on . . .			
	All problems	Most problems	Some problems	None of the problems
Wrote the information into a correct equation		✓		
Identified the unknown in the problem	✓			
Converted Celsius temperatures to Kelvin		✓		
Wrote the Charles's Law equation			✓	
Solved the equation for the unknown	✓			
Wrote all the numbers with correct unit labels	✓			

"rubrics," both in schools and on the Internet, that were actually quality rating scales for "criteria" that were more often aspects of the task than of learning.

Two, because quality ratings are judgments and not descriptions, they do not include information that will move learning forward. Quality ratings stop the action. They provide no information for, for example, a student who is "good" and wants to become "excellent," to help that student decide what to do next. And although excellent-good-fair-poor scales are more commonly the culprits in misguided uses of quality rating scales where rubrics are intended, language that sounds "standards based" can be co-opted into quality ratings as well. If the scale is just a list of words—like Advanced, Proficient, Nearing Proficient, Beginner—without descriptions, that's a rating scale. Or sometimes what look like "descriptions" really aren't. "Solves problems at an advanced level," "Solves problems at a proficient level," and so on, are just rating scales dolled up into sentences. These sentences do not contain any descriptive information about performance that will move learning forward.

Three, quality ratings often lure teachers into using task-based criteria because quality ratings are easy to apply to such criteria. For example, for a written report, task-based criteria might be Introduction, Text, Illustrations, and References. You just judge the quality—in effect, assign a grade—to each part of the task. In fact, quality rating scales used with schoolwork amount to the same thing as assigning grades without comments. Rubrics began to be popular in the 1980s as an antidote to this very thing. As educa-

> **SELF-REFLECTION**
>
> Can you identify any checklists or rating scales you use that you want to revise to become rubrics? Can you identify any rubrics you use that might be more effective if revised into checklists (for example, to lay out the requirements for an assignment)? How would you proceed with these revisions?

tors began to see performance assessment as a solution to the problem of too much minimum-competency testing, rubrics became the solution to the problem of the "just a number" results of such tests. To co-opt rubrics into quality rating scales does violence, in my mind, to the whole point and purpose of using rubrics in the first place.

Summing up

Why include a chapter on checklists and rating scales in a book about rubrics? I hope that after reading the chapter several reasons are clear. First, distinguishing checklists and rating scales from rubrics should make the characteristics of rubrics clearer. Rating scales often masquerade as rubrics, and I hope you can identify those and avoid them or revise them. Second, checklists and frequency rating scales have some important uses, on their own or in conjunction with rubrics. Checklists are great for helping students see whether they have followed directions, included all required elements of an assignment, adhered to format requirements, and the like. Frequency rating scales are good for assessing certain kinds of performance skills and for assessing behavior, work habits, and other learning skills. Finally, this chapter identified and defined quality rating scales, which are often mistaken for rubrics. Be on the lookout for those and stamp out their use whenever possible. They are Trojan horses that will allow old-fashioned grading judgments to slip in where rubrics were intended.

8

More Examples

This chapter contains more examples of rubrics in several different content areas and grade levels: elementary reading, middle school science, and high school technology education. I encourage you to read all the examples, even if the content or grade level is not one you currently teach.

Oral reading fluency

I especially like the example related to Figure 8.1. Several Title I reading teachers in a district I worked with used some version of it. Katrina Kimmell was a Title I reading teacher at West Hills Primary School in Kittanning, Pennsylvania, and the version of the rubric and student story I present here are from her classroom. The district's 1st grade students were working with a scripted curriculum that required monitoring progress in fluency on at least a weekly basis. Progress in fluency was monitored using words correct per minute. Thoughtful teachers knew that "oral reading fluency" should mean more to students than words correct per minute. Figure 8.1 presents the rubric.

It is worth noting that the rubric uses simple intensity scales: "no, a little, some, lots" and variations. These are words and concepts that Ms. Kimmell's young students understood. However, by themselves the words are open to much interpretation (how much is "some"?). Coupled with instruction, however, the points on the scale were clarified for

Figure 8.1   Oral Reading Fluency Rubric

ORAL READING FLUENCY RUBRIC				
Name: Daniel		Date:		
	1	**2**	**3**	**4**
Expression	No Expression	A little Expression	Some Expression	(Lots of) Expression
Phrasing	No Phrasing	A little Phrasing	Some Phrasing	Very Good Phrasing (4)
Speed	Way too slow or way too fast!	A little bit too slow or a little bit too fast.	Almost perfect but still needs practice...	Just Right! (4)

Source: Used with permission from Katrina D. Kimmell, West Hills Primary School, Kittanning, PA.

students simultaneously with the learning target (oral reading fluency) and the criteria (Expression, Phrasing, and Speed). Before using the rubrics for self-assessment, Ms. Kimmell shared the learning target with students, using the rubrics but also using modeling and demonstration. Here is what she did.

First, she explained the context. She told students they were going to practice reading. After practicing a few times, students taped their oral reading with a tape recorder. Then they evaluated their own performances using the Oral Reading Fluency Rubric.

Second, Ms. Kimmell explained the learning target and criteria for success. She did this by using the rubric, but also by modeling and demonstration. She showed students that the rubric has three different sections. Each section is something needed for students to become really good readers. The first one is Expression. She asked students, "What do you think that means? What does reading sound like when it has good expression?" Then she paused for class discussion.

The second criterion is Phrasing. The teacher explained that phrasing means that you don't read a sentence word by word like this (and modeled "robot reading"). Instead, you read a few words at a time—just like we sound when we are talking. Then she paused for class discussion and demonstrations of "robot reading" versus "reading like we talk."

The last criterion is Speed. Good reading is not so fast that no one can understand what you are reading, but not so slow that it's boring or you lose your place. Then the teacher went over the descriptions of top-level (4) performance in each category. The students practiced reading, then taped themselves after practice. Finally, the students used the Oral Reading Fluency Rubric to assess their own performance.

Before reading, Daniel, the boy whose example is shown, looked at a chart to see how many correct words per minute he had read the previous week and found that it was 51. Ms. Kimmell told him that she wanted him to try to read at least 53 words this time, but he said he wanted to try for 61. She said, "That would be great, but anything over 53 would be a good job." He and the teacher discussed strategies he could use, like finger tracking and sounding out words. Then when he read his passage, he read 61 correct words per minute—and said, "I told you I would."

Daniel's self-assessment in Figure 8.1, coupled with the questions he asked and his response to his success, suggest that learning how to read fluently was a target that he understood. The rubric helped him engage with the target according to specific criteria and helped him interpret his success as more multidimensional than just a words-per-minute score.

Science laboratory reports

In an 8th grade science inclusion classroom, the regular and special education teachers worked together. They wanted their students to learn science inquiry process skills—how to write testable questions and hypotheses and gather and interpret data to answer them—as well as how to write up the process in a conventional lab report. The teachers prepared a handout, "How to Write a Lab Report," and the rubric shown in Figure 8.2, which they adapted from Internet sources. They also taught lessons about lab reports that included having students look at sample lab reports before they began work on their own. During their work, the teachers gave students information and coaching on the science content (in this case, filtering water) and necessary materials. After students completed their lab reports but before they turned them in, they used the rubric for self-assessment and potential revisions.

Figure 8.2   Science Laboratory Report Rubric

	4	3	2	1
Introduction—Stating Research Questions and Hypotheses	States a hypothesis that is based on research and/or sound reasoning and is testable. Report title reflects question or hypothesis.	States a hypothesis that is based on research and/or sound reasoning and is testable. Report title may not reflect the question or hypothesis.	States a hypothesis, although basis for the hypothesis is not clear or hypothesis is not testable. Report title may not reflect the question or hypothesis.	Does not state a hypothesis. Introduction may be a general statement of the topic or the assignment, or may be missing or unclear.
Procedure—Designing the Experiment	Procedure includes a very detailed description or step-by-step list of how the experiment was performed. All steps are included.	Procedure includes a very detailed description or step-by-step list of how the experiment was performed; however, all steps are not included.	Description or step-by-step list of how the experiment was performed is vague, and experiment would be hard for someone else to duplicate.	Description is unclear, and experiment could not be repeated because of lack of description.
Results—Collecting Data	Results and data are accurately recorded, organized so it is easy for the reader to see trends. All appropriate labels are included.	Results are clear and labeled. Trends are not obvious.	Results are unclear, missing labels, and trends are not obvious at all.	Results may be present, but too disorganized or poorly recorded to make sense of.

continued

Figure 8.2   Science Laboratory Report Rubric *(continued)*

	4	3	2	1
Analyzing Data	The data and observations are analyzed accurately. Trends are noted. Enough data were taken to establish conclusion.	Analysis is somewhat lacking in insight. There is enough data, although additional data would be more powerful.	Analysis is lacking in insight. Not enough data were gathered to establish trends, or analysis does not follow the data.	Analysis is inaccurate and based on insufficient data.
Interpreting Results and Drawing Conclusions	Summarizes data used to draw logical conclusions about hypothesis. Discusses real-world applications of findings.	Summarizes data used to draw conclusions about hypothesis. Some logic or real-world application may be unclear.	Conclusions about hypothesis are not derived from data. Some logic or real-world application may be unclear.	No conclusions about hypothesis are evident. Logic and application of findings are missing.

Source: Used with permission.

After using the rubric, the special education teacher reflected on the experience. Most of his students, he said, "had a greater understanding of what constituted good-quality work" and "a clear picture of what was expected." Students who did this were able to compare their work with the criteria and performance descriptions in the rubric and, based on that comparison, make decisions about how to improve their work. In addition, they took greater responsibility for their own learning.

One group did not meet expectations on every criterion, but even for that group the rubric was helpful. The rubric allowed both teacher and students to identify the one area (drawing and expressing conclusions that follow from the data) to work on. From this perspective, the rubric was helpful even for unsuccessful work because it furnished the information needed for the students' next steps.

Welding

Technology education is an important content area that is outside my own teaching background and experience. Andrew Rohwedder is a technology education teacher at Richardton-Taylor High School in Richardton, North Dakota. Figure 8.3 presents Mr. Rohwedder's welding rubric.

The welding rubric is an excellent example of a well-constructed rubric. It is clear and descriptive. It can be shared with students and would support learning and formative assessment, especially student self-assessment, as well as grading.

Because technology education is not a content area I know anything about, I was able to read this rubric as a new learner would. If that is the case for you, consider how well-constructed rubrics clarify the learning target. When I first read the rubric, I was able to envision what a good weld would look like.

I also had a question. Two of the criteria seemed to be about appearance (Weld Width and Height, and Appearance). And yet, given how well the rubric was designed, I doubted that Mr. Rohwedder had simply written the same thing twice. So I asked him what the difference was between those two criteria, and I learned some more about welding.

He said, "The width of a weld will depend on many factors controlled by the welder. Usually the width of a weld is proportional to the thickness of the metal and how the joint is prepared. The height of the weld will depend on the heat and amount of filler material laid down by the welder. Once again this is determined by the parent material and joint preparation and type of joint. The appearance of a weld should be smooth, uniform, and chipped free of slag."

Figure 8.3   Welding Rubric

	Advanced 4 points	Proficient 3 points	Basic 2 points	Below Basic 1 point	Total Points
Slag removed 100% All slag chipped. Weld bead is clean.	Bead is clean, has been chipped and wire-brushed.	Bead is somewhat clean. Minimum slag at the edges of the bead.	Bead needs major chipping and brushing.	Shows little care about quality.	
Weld width and height 100% Uniform width and thickness throughout the entire length of each weld.	Bead is uniform width all along the length of each weld. Has a smooth appearance.	Bead maintains width and length. Shows some small blemishes along the weld.	Not a uniform thickness throughout the weld. Thickness goes to extremes.	Weld is cut off in places, not uniform along the weld. Shows bare spots.	
Appearance 100% Smooth, with uniform dense ripples; doesn't show the bead traveling too fast or slow.	Weld shows a constant speed and uniformity the entire length.	Weld shows a constant speed with some blemishes that are minimal.	Weld shows definite areas of speeding up and slowing down. Ripples tend to be coarse.	Weld has been done too fast or too slow. Weld is not complete. Trapped impurities in the weld.	
Face of bead 100% Convex, free of voids and high spots, shows uniformity throughout the bead.	Has a nice rounded look. Is not overly high, or low. Bead covers a wide area of each weld.	Bead is well rounded, mostly uniform over the length of the weld. Shows some high spots and low spots.	Bead shows many high and low areas. Total lack of uniformity throughout the weld.	Weld does not blend into one single bead.	

	Advanced 4 points	Proficient 3 points	Basic 2 points	Below Basic 1 point	Total Points
Edge of bead 100% Good fusion, no overlapping or undercutting.	Sides and edges are smooth, blending into each weld. Undercutting is kept to a minimum. Weld does not float on surface.	Moderately smooth blending. Undercutting and float are present. Strength of the weld is still strong.	Float and undercut are very apparent. Weld lacks strength and flow.	Metal is burned through. Weld has no connection to metal.	
Beginning and ending full size 100% Crater well filled.	End of each weld is complete; the line doesn't taper off.	Weld ending is full but shows some tapering and a crater present.	Crater distinctly present at the end of the bead.	Metal is burned through at the end.	
Surrounding plate 100% Welding surface free of spatter.	Spatter is kept to a minimum.	Some spatter is present but not displeasing.	Spatter is in large amounts.	Spatter takes away from the integrity of the weld.	
Penetration 100% Complete without burn-through.	Weld penetrates deep into the metal and adds strength and fusion to the edges and depth.	Weld penetrates deep but does not resurface through the bottom of a jointed weld.	Weld is uneven in depth, lacks uniformity along weld length.	Weld floats on top of the metal. Has no strength.	

Source: Used with permission from Andrew Rohwedder, Technology Educator, Richardton-Taylor High School, Richardton, ND.

For me, this interchange was an object lesson in one of the main points this book is trying to make. Good rubrics help clarify the learning target for students (or anyone else who does not yet have a clear vision of it, like me with welding). Good rubrics become a foundation for learning and formative assessment as well as for grading. Most important, good rubrics are tools the students can use to help themselves learn.

Summing up

SELF-REFLECTION

What is your current thinking about rubrics after reading Part I of this book? How does it compare with your thinking from the first self-reflection, before you began to read?

This book is full of examples, but I think you almost can't have too many! Chapter 2 included the counterexample "My State Poster" rubric. Chapter 3 showed the silly example of a rubric for laughing and the example of the life-cycle project rubric, a work-in-progress that illustrated how you might approach revising and improving rubrics. Chapter 4 included examples of general rubrics for foundational skills: the 6+1 Trait Writing rubrics, student-friendly rubrics for mathematics problem solving, and rubrics for report writing and for creativity. Chapter 5 presented some examples of task-specific rubrics, and Chapter 6 contained examples of general and specific proficiency-based rubrics for understanding the concept of area and its relationship to multiplication and division. Chapter 7 contained examples of checklists and rating scales, both to demonstrate their usefulness in their own right and to show by contrast how they are not rubrics. This chapter added three more examples to the mix, in elementary reading, middle school science, and high school technology education.

My hope is that from this collection of examples, you can by induction generalize the characteristics of good rubrics yourself. Lay your conclusions beside what I have listed as the characteristics of good rubrics in the book and—I hope!—see that they match. At this point, then, you should have a firm idea of what effective rubrics look like.

This chapter concludes Part 1 of the book, which was about the various types of rubrics (and, in Chapter 7, the related tools—checklists and rating scales) and how to write them. Part 2 explains how to use rubrics. I hope that as you explore the different uses of rubrics, you will see more and more why it is important to emphasize the two defining factors of appropriate criteria and descriptions of performance along a continuum of quality. These elements are the genius of rubrics because they are the "active ingredients" in all of the uses described in Part 2.

Part 2

How to Use
RUBRICS

Rubrics and Formative Assessment: Sharing Learning Targets with Students

Learning targets describe what the student is going to learn, in language that the student can understand and aim for during today's lesson (Moss & Brookhart, 2012). Learning targets include criteria that students can use to judge how close they are to the target, and that is why rubrics (or parts of rubrics, depending on the focus of the lesson) are good vehicles for sharing learning targets with students.

The idea that students will learn better if *they* know what they are supposed to learn is so important! Most teacher preparation programs emphasize *instructional objectives*, which are a great planning tool for teachers. However, instructional objectives are written in teacher language ("The student will be able to . . ."). Not only are the students referred to in third person, but the statements about what they will be able to do are in terms of evidence for teachers. In contrast, learning targets must imply the evidence that *students* should be looking for. Sometimes, for simple targets, instructional objectives can be turned into learning targets by simply making them first-person ("I will know I have learned this when I can   "). More often, however, the language of the evidentiary part of the learning target—what students will look for—also needs to be written and demonstrated in terms students will understand. After all, if most of your students understand what your instructional objective means, you probably don't need to teach the lesson.

The most powerful way to share with students a vision of what they are supposed to be learning is to make sure your instructional activities and formative assessments (and, later, your summative assessments) are *performances of understanding*. A performance of understanding embodies the learning target in what you ask students to actually do. To use a simple, concrete example, if you want students to be able to use their new science content vocabulary to explain meiosis, design an activity in which students have to use the terms in explanations. That would be a performance of understanding. A word-search activity would not be a performance of understanding for that learning target because what the students would actually be doing is recognizing the words.

Performances of understanding *show* students, by what they ask of them, what it is they are supposed to be learning. Performances of understanding *develop* that learning through the students' experience doing the work. Finally, performances of understanding *give evidence* of students' learning by providing work that is available for inspection by both teacher and student. Not every performance of understanding uses rubrics. For those that do, however, rubrics support all three functions (showing, developing, and giving evidence of learning).

> ## SELF-REFLECTION
>
> How do you share learning targets with your students? Do you ever use rubrics as part of this communication? Besides giving the students the rubrics, what do you do? What have you learned from doing this?

How to use rubrics to share learning targets and criteria for success

Use rubrics to share learning targets and criteria for success with students when the learning target requires thinking, writing, analyzing, demonstrating complex skills, or constructing complex products. These are the kinds of learning targets for which checklists or other simple devices cannot fully represent the learning outcomes you intend students to reach. This section presents several strategies for using rubrics to develop in students' minds a conception of what it is they are supposed to learn and the criteria by which they will know to what degree they have learned it. Use one or more of these strategies, or design your own.

Ask students to pose clarifying questions about the rubrics

If rubrics are well constructed, and if students understand the performance criteria and quality levels encoded into them, then the Proficient level of the rubrics describes what learning looks like. An obvious but often overlooked strategy for finding out how students think about anything, including rubrics, is to ask them what is puzzling (Chappuis & Stiggins, 2002; Moss & Brookhart, 2009). Here is an organized way to do that:

- *Give students copies of the rubrics.* Ask them, in pairs, to discuss what the rubrics mean, proceeding one criterion at a time.
- *As they talk, have them write down questions.* These should be questions the pairs are not able to resolve themselves.
- *Try to resolve the questions with peers.* Put two or three pairs together for groups of four or six. Again, students write down any questions they still can't resolve.
- *Collect the final list of questions and discuss them as a whole group.* Sometimes these questions will illuminate unfamiliar terms or concepts, or unfamiliar attributes of work. Sometimes the questions will illuminate a lack of clarity in the rubrics and result in editing the rubrics.

Ask students to state the rubrics in their own words

The classic comprehension activity is to put something in your own words. Reading teachers have beginning readers retell stories. Teachers at all grade levels give students directions and, to check for understanding, say, "What are you going to do?" Friends and relatives, when finding you cannot tell them what they said, become justifiably annoyed and snap, "Weren't you listening?" Asking students to state the rubrics in their own words is more than just finding "student-friendly language." It is a comprehension activity. Having students state rubrics in their own words will help them understand the rubrics and will give you evidence of their understanding.

Below are several ways to have students state rubrics in their own words. Select the one that fits your students' needs and the content you are teaching. Or, inspired by one of these methods, design your own.

Rubric translator. Put students together in pairs and give them your rubrics. If possible, also provide them with a sample of work at each level. Give them a blank template that matches the rubrics you gave them, which will look like an empty chart. Alternatively, you can use a worksheet like the example in Figure 9.1. Fill in the top row

Figure 9.1   **Rubric "Translator" Template**

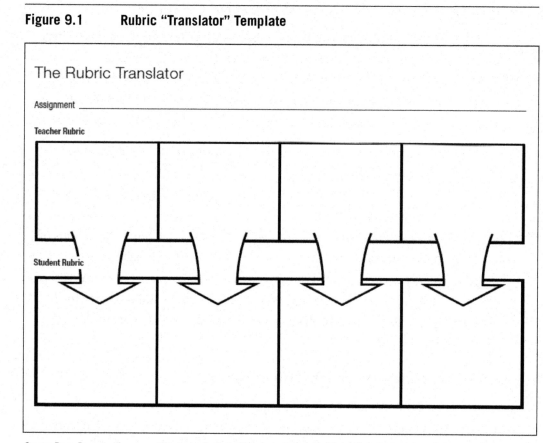

Source: From *Formative Assessment Strategies for Every Classroom,* 2nd ed. (p. 90), by Susan M. Brookhart, 2010, Alexandria, VA: ASCD. Copyright 2010 by ASCD. Reprinted with permission.

and have the students write in the bottom row. You will need one diagram like this for each criterion.

Have students discuss each criterion in turn, using these questions or other similar questions appropriate to the rubrics under consideration:

- *How many criteria are there?* This question ensures students can find the criteria on the rubric.

- *What are the names of each criterion, and what do these words mean?* This question focuses the students on the meaning of the criteria as traits or qualities before they begin writing.

- *For each criterion in turn, going one at a time, read the descriptions of work along the whole range of progress.* Discuss what elements are described and how they change from level to level. For each criterion, students should do this for the range of performance-level descriptions before they start to write.

- *Put the level descriptions in your own words, varying the same elements from level to level as the teacher's rubrics did.* Students should discuss the wording with their partners until they agree on what to write.
- *If work samples have been provided, do the new "translated" rubrics still match the work at the intended levels?* This is a check on the rephrasing, so that students can make sure their translations preserved the original meaning.

Ready-steady-pair-share. Moss and Brookhart (2012) describe this strategy for having students discuss rubrics in their own words in order to understand their learning targets and criteria for success. This strategy begins with understanding the rubrics and carries through their use with a single performance. Here are the steps involved:

- *Give a rubric to students before you give them an assignment.* The assignment should be a performance of understanding; that is, it should be a clear instance of demonstrating the knowledge and skills that you intend for students to learn.
- *In pairs, students take turns explaining the rubric to their partners.* This step lasts until the students think they understand how the rubric applies to their work on the assignment they are about to do.
- *Students begin the assignment.* Students do not need to remain in their "rubric pairs" to work but should work on the assignment however it is designed—individually, in other groups, or whatever.
- *Halfway through the assignment, students return to their rubric partners and explain how what they are doing meets the criteria and performance levels they discussed at the beginning.* Students may question each other about their work and their explanations.
- *Students finish the assignment.* Students go back to work individually or in their work groups, however the assignment is designed.
- *When students have finished the assignment, they return to their rubric partners and explain how what they have done meets the criteria and desired performance level.* After partners are satisfied with each other's explanations, students turn in the work. They may turn in the results of this final peer evaluation as well.

Student co-constructed rubrics. Involving students in constructing rubrics is an excellent way to help them feel ownership of both their learning in general and their achievement or accomplishment on specific assignments and assessments and to help them learn more at the same time. The reason is that the criteria for good work are part of the broader concept of what it means to know and be able to do something.

Different procedures have been described for co-constructing rubrics (Andrade, Du, & Mycek, 2010; Arter & Chappuis, 2006; Nitko & Brookhart, 2011). Having students co-construct rubrics is like the bottom-up method of developing general rubrics described in Chapter 3, using student input. The balance between the amount of student direction and the amount of teacher guidance will vary. For some very familiar skills, student input can furnish all or most of the ideas needed for identifying criteria and performance-level descriptions, and the teacher can be a facilitator. For less familiar skills, student input can be part of a dialogue with the teacher. Teacher guidance will come in the form of asking probing questions of students and also contributing ideas to the mix.

Therefore, the steps below for student co-construction of rubrics are a generalization of the major actions different authors have described. These steps need to be adapted to the students' content knowledge and skills and to their familiarity with the content and with rubric development. In some cases, the teacher may add information or suggestions; in others, the students can do most of the process themselves. I have used different versions myself, depending on these aspects of the context.

- *Identify the content knowledge and skills the rubrics will be assessing.* For co-constructed rubrics, the knowledge and skills should be something students are already somewhat familiar with—for example, writing an effective term paper that requires library and Internet research.
- *Give students some sample work.* Have students review the work. For short pieces of writing—for example, a brief essay—the work can be read aloud. Or students can look over the examples in pairs or small groups.
- *Students brainstorm their responses to the work in terms of strengths and weaknesses.* The more specific the responses are, the better. For example, "The report answered all my questions about stars and raised some new ones I hadn't thought of" is more specific than "It was a good report"; or "I didn't understand the explanation of how stable stars burn" is more specific than "The report wasn't clear."
- *Students categorize the strengths and weaknesses in terms of the attributes they describe.* The teacher may have to guide students here so the attributes are not attributes of the *task* (for example, cover, introduction, body, references) but rather aspects of the *learning* that was supposed to occur (for example, understanding of the content, communication of the content, clarity and completeness of explanation, and so on).
- *Further discussion and wordsmithing of the attribute categories continue until there is agreement on criteria for the rubric.* Attributes can be grouped and ungrouped until

they express criteria at the appropriate level of generality. Attributes that are not important for the learning to be assessed may be removed from the list of criteria. For example, handwriting may be an attribute that was noted but, upon discussion, found to be unrelated to the content and skills the rubrics are concentrating on.

- *For each criterion, students discuss what elements should be described and how they might change from performance level to performance level.* As this discussion proceeds, record the results as drafts of descriptions of performance at each level. One effective way of drafting performance-level descriptions is to start with the description of ideal work and "back down" the quality for each level below it. The "rubric machine" in Figure 9.2, or something like it, may help with this. A separate template of this sort is needed for each criterion.
- *When students arrive at a draft rubric, they apply it to the original work samples.* Additional work samples may be used here as well. Students note where questions arise and use these observations to revise the rubric.

Ask students to match samples of work to rubrics

Matching samples of work to rubrics is one way of building up by induction student concepts of what the criteria mean. Identifying attributes and distinguishing examples from nonexamples are classic concept-development strategies.

Sorting work. Give students rubrics for an assignment demonstrating the knowledge and skills students are about to learn. Also give students several examples of work ranging from very poor to very good. Students sort work according to the criteria and performance-level descriptions in the rubrics. When students see several different examples of the same criteria, they begin to generalize meaning. They can begin to separate critical defining attributes of the criteria. For example, for the criterion of understanding planetary orbits, students might observe a critical attribute to be that the planets are placed in their appropriate orbits in a model of the solar system. They will begin to distinguish critical attributes of the work from irrelevant attributes. For example, what the model planets are made out of might be an irrelevant attribute, as some perhaps are made out of modeling clay and others are made out of papier-mâché. Students should discuss the attributes they are focusing on, and why, to help solidify their concepts of the criteria and performance levels.

Clear and cloudy. As an extension of sorting work according to the various performance-level descriptions, you can ask students to identify which pieces of work they had no trouble identifying with a particular level of a given criterion ("clear") and which

Figure 9.2   Template for Student-Constructed Rubrics

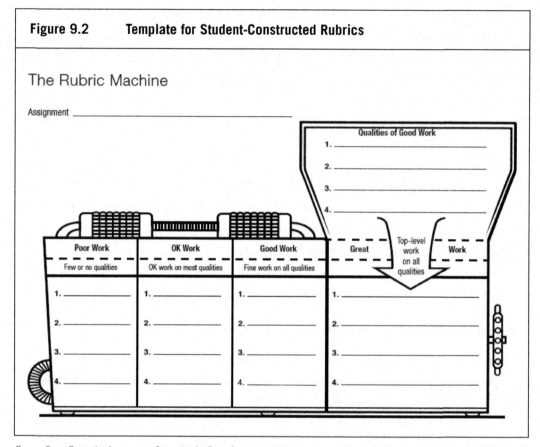

The Rubric Machine

Assignment _____

Qualities of Good Work
1. _____
2. _____
3. _____
4. _____

Poor Work	OK Work	Good Work	Great	Top-level work on all qualities	Work
Few or no qualities	OK work on most qualities	Fine work on all qualities			
1. _____	1. _____	1. _____	1. _____		
2. _____	2. _____	2. _____	2. _____		
3. _____	3. _____	3. _____	3. _____		
4. _____	4. _____	4. _____	4. _____		

Source: From *Formative Assessment Strategies for Every Classroom,* 2nd ed. (p. 86), by Susan M. Brookhart, 2010, Alexandria, VA: ASCD. Copyright 2010 by ASCD. Reprinted with permission.

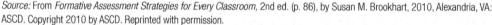

pieces of work were difficult to evaluate or identify with a particular level of a given crite-rion ("cloudy"). Then discuss, again in pairs, small groups, or whole group, the reasons for these designations. The "clear" and "cloudy" designations and discussion will illumi-nate what the criteria mean and how students are understanding them.

Highlighters or colored pencils. Students use highlighters or colored pencils to mark qualities described in the rubrics and on sample work. For example, if the rubric says "Identifies the author's purpose and supports this conclusion with details from the text," the student would highlight this statement in the rubrics and at the location in his paper identifying the author's purpose and supporting details. Students learn what the criteria and performance-level descriptions mean by locating and reviewing specific instances in the work. A version of this activity can also be used with the students' own papers for formative assessment (see Chapter 10). When used with sample work before students have begun their own work, students can talk about what they highlighted and why in pairs, small groups, or as a whole class. Comments from these discussions can be used as an introduction to the knowledge and skills students will be learning.

Explore and teach one criterion at a time

To introduce students to criteria for new learning targets, handle one criterion at a time (Arter & Chappuis, 2006; Moss & Brookhart, 2009). Adapt any of the previous strategies to one criterion, setting aside the others for the time being, or use one of the following strategies.

Strategic goal setting. Give students a rubric before they do an activity or assignment. Address one criterion at a time, with a minilesson if the concept is new. Ask students to plan a separate strategy for successful performance on that criterion. Have them record their strategies right on their copies of the rubric. When work on the activity or assignment begins, have students use their rubrics, annotated with their personal strategies, to monitor and regulate their work.

Coming to terms. Rubrics often contain terms that are new to students. In small groups, have students read all the performance-level descriptions for one criterion and make a list of all the unfamiliar words in the descriptions, at any level, for that criterion. Then have students define, describe, and find examples of those terms. If the listing of words is done in groups, the groups can exchange their lists to do the definitions, descriptions, and examples. Alternatively, a merged list can be created, and then one or several terms can be assigned to each group. They can share their definitions, descriptions, and examples as class presentations or small-group presentations.

Summing up

This chapter has explored ways to use rubrics for sharing learning targets and criteria for success with students. This is the first, and foundational, strategy for formative assessment. It is also a foundational strategy for effective instruction. Although rubrics are not the only way to communicate to students what they are about to learn, they are an excellent resource for doing so. Rubrics make especially good vehicles for sharing learning targets when the target is complex and not just a matter of recall of information. The reason is that rubrics bring together sets of relevant criteria. The nature of a complex understanding or skill is that several qualities must operate at one time.

10

Rubrics and Formative Assessment: Feedback and Student Self-Assessment

Formative assessment is an active and intentional learning process that partners the teacher and students to continuously and systematically gather evidence of learning with the express goal of improving student achievement (Moss & Brookhart, 2009, p. 6). Formative assessment is about *forming* learning—that is, it is assessment that gives information that moves students forward. If no further learning occurred, then whatever the intention, an assessment was not formative.

SELF-REFLECTION

How do you use rubrics for feedback and student self-assessment in your classroom?

Chapter 9 described how to use rubrics to help clarify learning targets for students—the foundational strategy of formative assessment. This chapter covers the use of rubrics for giving feedback that feeds forward, for supporting student self-assessment and goal setting, and for helping students ask effective questions about their work.

How to use rubrics for teacher and peer feedback

Because rubrics enumerate the criteria for learning and describe performance along a continuum for each one, they are a good framework for feedback. This section presents several strategies for using rubrics as the basis for teacher and peer feedback. Use one of them or design similar strategies that work in your context.

Teacher feedback on rubrics-based feedback sheets

If you are using well-written, general, analytic rubrics (as I recommend for most purposes) for sharing with students and for feedback, you can photocopy the rubrics themselves, leaving space for comments. Provide feedback by circling the performance level for each criterion that best matches the student's work in its current form. Then you will not have to rewrite the general description, which is already circled. Instead, use what time you have available for written feedback to write something specific to the student's work.

For example, if the class is working on the ideas in their writing, the teacher may give feedback on writing using the Ideas rubric in the 6+1 Trait Writing rubrics (see Appendix A). If she has circled "Support for topic is incidental or confusing, not focused," the specific comments might tell the student what she found confusing or why the supporting details did not seem, in fact, to support the topic. This combination of general feedback from the rubric and specific feedback in writing will be enough for many students to see the way forward and improve their work in revision. For a few students, if conferencing is needed—for example, if the teacher wants to ask a student about the logic of including some details or check for understanding of story details that seemed confusing—much of the preliminary information is already present in the circled portions of the general rubrics and in the specific written feedback.

Yellow and blue make green

Similar to the "highlighters or colored pencils" method presented in Chapter 9 for helping students understand the learning target and criteria they are aiming for, you can also use highlighters for teacher feedback on student work and student self-assessment. Ask students to use the highlighters as before, highlighting a statement from the description of performance in the rubric and highlighting where they identify this quality, but this time in their own work instead of in sample work. They can then assess whether they are satisfied with the evidence they have highlighted or want to change, augment, or revise it.

Two-color highlighting (Chappuis, 2009) can be used to compare teacher and self-assessment perspectives on the same work. Students use yellow highlighters, and teachers use blue highlighters. Where there is agreement on what constitutes evidence for performance as described in the rubric, the resulting highlights will be green.

This is not just a coloring-book exercise, however. Important information comes with the comparison. If most of the highlighted area is green, both the student and the teacher are interpreting the work in the same way and more or less agreeing on its quality. If most of the highlighted area is yellow, the student is seeing evidence that the teacher is not. It may be that the student is not clear on the meaning of the criterion, or the student may be overvaluing the work. If most of the highlighted area is blue, the teacher is seeing evidence that the student is not. The student may be not clear on the meaning of the criterion or undervaluing the work.

Any place where teacher and student perspectives vary on the worth of the student's work relative to criteria can be fertile ground for written feedback from the teacher, student questioning, or conferencing. The feedback, questions, or conferences should address more than just understanding the highlighting or the description of current work. What should come next? Provide feedback on what the student can do to improve the work.

Paired-peer feedback

Peers can use rubrics to give each other feedback. The rubrics provide structure for peer discussions, making it easier for the students to focus on the criteria rather than personal reactions to the work. The rubrics also aid dialogue. As the students use the language of the rubrics to discuss each other's work, they are developing their own conceptions of the meaning of the criteria while they are giving information to their peers.

The simplest form of peer feedback involves students working in pairs. The teacher should assign peers that are well matched in terms of interest, ability, or compatibility, depending on the particular assignment.

Peer feedback works best in a classroom where constructive criticism is viewed as an important part of learning. In a classroom characterized by a grading-focused or evaluative culture ("Whad-ja-get?"), peer feedback may not work well; students may hesitate to criticize their peers so as not to imply there is anything "wrong." Try peer feedback only when you are sure that your students value opportunities to learn. If you try peer feedback and it doesn't work very well, even after careful preparation, be prepared to ask yourself whether your students are telling you they are more focused on getting a good grade than improving their work.

Assuming that you have a learning-focused classroom culture, you still need to prepare students for peer feedback. Make sure that the students understand the rubrics they will be using and that they can apply them to anonymous work samples accurately. Make sure the students understand the assignments on which they will be using the rubrics for the peer feedback. Set a few important ground rules and have students explain, and even role-play, what they mean. Use rules that make sense for your grade level, students, and content area. Here are examples of some common peer-feedback ground rules:

When You Are Giving Peer Feedback
1. Read or view your peer's work carefully. Talk about the work, not the person who did the work.
2. Use terms from the rubrics to explain and describe what you see in the work.
3. Give your own suggestions and ideas, and explain why you think these suggestions would help improve the work.
4. Listen to your peer's comments and questions.

When You Are Receiving Peer Feedback
1. Listen to your peer's comments. Take time to think about them before you respond.
2. Compare your peer's comments to the rubrics, and decide what comments you will use in your revisions.
3. Thank your peer for the feedback.

Finally, peer feedback gets better with practice. When you use paired-peer feedback, observe the pairs and give them feedback on their feedback, as it were. Look for, and comment on, how students use the rubrics, how clearly they describe the work, how useful their suggestions for improvement are, how supportive they are, and so on. Just as for any skill, giving and receiving peer feedback can (and should) be taught and learned.

How to use rubrics for student self-assessment and goal setting

Because rubrics encode the qualities of good work that students are shooting for, they are the appropriate reference point for students' monitoring of their own work.

This section presents some examples of how that might be done, and I encourage you to devise others that fit the students, content, and grade level you teach.

Strategic goal setting revisited

In Chapter 9 we talked about students using rubrics to plan a separate strategy for successful performance on each criterion and recording their strategies on their copies of the rubric. When work on the activity or assignment begins, have students use their rubrics, annotated with their personal strategies, to monitor and regulate their work. They can use any number of methods for this. Here are a couple of them.

Quick-check. Each time students work on their assignments or projects, set aside one minute at the end of work time. For each strategy students have identified, have them check the following:

- Did I do this today?
- Did it help me?

For example, consider a student in a writing class that was using the 6+1 Trait Writing rubrics. One student's strategy for improving his performance (and learning) under the Word Choice criterion was "I will check a thesaurus any time a word isn't as powerful, precise, or engaging as I would like." Thus the student would ask himself, "Did I use a thesaurus in my writing today? Did it help me choose more powerful, precise, or engaging words?" Students can make their own charts to record these checks, or they can make a mark next to where they have written their strategies on their rubrics.

Journaling. In classes where regular journaling is part of student self-reflection, students can record their strategies and their reflections upon the use of those strategies as part of their regular self-reflection. Here the questions are similar—Did I actually use the strategy I planned to and did it help me improve my work?—but there is room for reflecting on what specifically the strategy helped (or did not help) the student do and why that might be the case. Teachers may or may not read these reflections. The intent is for students to exercise metacognition, to think about their thinking.

Think-pair-don't share. Give students five minutes at the end of a work session to work in pairs. Each partner will describe the strategies that were planned, whether the strategies were used, to what degree the strategies helped, and why this might be so. This activity is a sort of debriefing of the work session, strategy use, and perceptions of learning. Similar to the conventional think-pair-share activity, students work with partners for this self-reflection session. Unlike a conventional think-pair-share activity, however, students do not share the results of their paired conversations with the whole class. The teacher may speak with one or more of the pairs as they are reflecting, to help them focus, as needed.

Charting progress

Charting progress means two different things. Students think of their progress toward completing individual assignments or projects, and they think of progress more broadly as learning. It is a good idea to have students chart at least the latter (learning progress) and sometimes the former.

Charting progress on an individual assignment, with rubrics. Give students the rubrics. Midway through the work, ask them to mark the rubrics at the level where they are for each criterion. Students can place a vertical line or a large dot at the appropriate level on each criterion. This can be done individually or in pairs. When the assignment or project is finished but before students turn it in, ask them to self-assess their finished product with the rubrics. Then have them draw an arrow from the first dot or line to the second, right on the rubrics, to make a graphic illustration of their progress.

Charting longer-term learning progress. General rubrics that are used across tasks can be used for longer-term charting of progress during a report period, a semester, or even a year. Depending on the purpose, students can use general rubrics for foundational skills (Chapter 4) or standards-based grading rubrics (Chapter 6) to keep track of their learning of those skills or standards. Have students construct a histogram with time on the horizontal axis and performance levels on the vertical axis.

Figure 10.1 gives an example of one student tracking her progress on the criterion "Writing an Explanation" in the Math Problem-Solving Rubric in Figure 4.1. Additional charts would be needed for the other criteria in the rubric. Each performance is listed, and then the student colors the bars in the graph to the height corresponding to her developing ability to show mathematical knowledge.

I want to make several very important points right away, because such a chart is prone to misinterpretation in classrooms that are grade oriented rather than learning oriented. First, this chart is for formative assessment and represents the student's practice and learning. It does *not* represent final outcomes, except perhaps that the last entry recorded shows the answer to the question "Where am I now?" The entries would not be averaged or otherwise summarized into a grade. This chart is the student's way of keeping track of her progress as she is learning. She will eventually receive a grade from a summative assessment of mathematical knowledge.

Figure 10.1   Example of Charting Progress with Rubrics

WRITING AN EXPLANATION

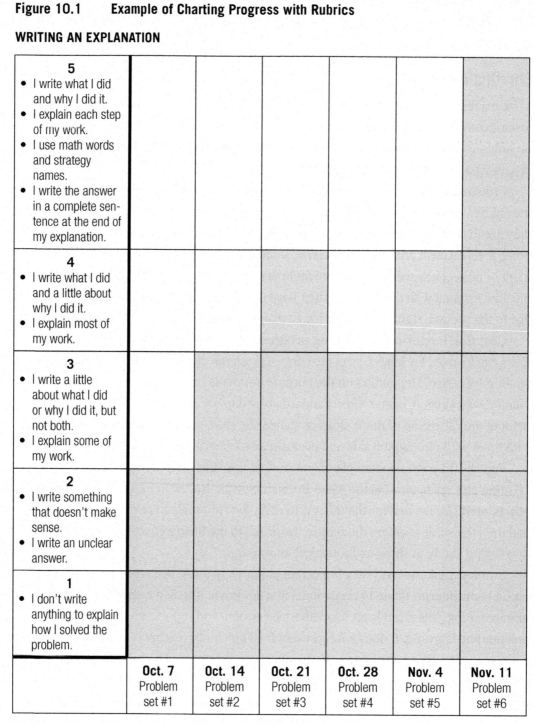

	Oct. 7 Problem set #1	Oct. 14 Problem set #2	Oct. 21 Problem set #3	Oct. 28 Problem set #4	Nov. 4 Problem set #5	Nov. 11 Problem set #6
5 • I write what I did and why I did it. • I explain each step of my work. • I use math words and strategy names. • I write the answer in a complete sentence at the end of my explanation.						
4 • I write what I did and a little about why I did it. • I explain most of my work.						
3 • I write a little about what I did or why I did it, but not both. • I explain some of my work.						
2 • I write something that doesn't make sense. • I write an unclear answer.						
1 • I don't write anything to explain how I solved the problem.						

Note: This example uses the Math Problem-Solving Rubric shown in Figure 4.1.

Second, the assessments or learning opportunities themselves are not "equal," and it is therefore mathematically inappropriate to summarize this chart by averaging. What is constant is the existence of the descriptions of performance for the various levels of Writing an Explanation, which are shown on the vertical axis. These performance levels describe the student's "steps" in learning. The assessments are simply opportunities for the student to practice, learn, and show what she knows. The purpose of the chart is for the student to see a learning curve. Bars that rise indicate progress. Bars that stay the same or fall indicate lack of progress. The graphic representation helps students focus on the performance levels and plan their next steps.

How to use rubrics to help students ask effective questions about their work

The genius of rubrics lies in their two main features: the criteria and descriptions of performance across a range of quality levels. The "main ideas" students need in order to understand quality are named by the criteria themselves. The elements in the descriptions flesh out these criteria with "supporting ideas" or aspects of the work that contribute to overall quality. Both of these help students ask effective questions about their work.

Simple self-reflection with rubrics

For experienced, self-regulated learners, simply give students dedicated time for self-reflection at designated points during their work, and ask them to use the rubrics to do it. Appropriate points in the work will vary. For writing, they come after the first draft and after subsequent revisions. For multipart projects, they come as different components of the project are drafted. For term papers, they come after each phase has been attempted (draft thesis or research question, library/Internet research, outline, writing of sections of the paper, and so on). Effective, self-regulated students can use rubrics to ask themselves whether their work contains the qualities they are shooting for. Many, if not most, students need more scaffolding and structure in order to use rubrics to ask effective questions about their work.

Scaffolded self-reflection with rubrics

Rubrics with structure like the Math Problem-Solving Rubric in Figure 4.1 make asking effective questions about work very straightforward. Ask students to focus first on the top category (or the category they are shooting for, if not the top one), and turn the elements into questions:

- Do I figure out the correct answer?
- Do I solve the problem with no mistakes?
- Do I use all the important information from the problem? [and so on]

For rubrics that do not use such straightforward, student-friendly terms, you can do one of two things. You can construct student-friendly rubrics with the students, with the constraint that the descriptions have to be "I" statements that can be turned into "Do I" questions. That exercise in itself is good for helping students learn exactly what their target is (see Chapter 9).

Alternatively, you can have students use the criteria and descriptive elements in rubrics to pose their own questions. For example, Level 4 of the Content category in the rubric for written projects in Figure 4.2 says:

> The thesis is clear. A large amount and variety of material and evidence support the thesis. All material is relevant. This material includes details. Information is accurate. Appropriate sources were consulted.

Brainstorm with students how questions can be written from these statements. If you start with "The thesis is clear," students might suggest questions such as these:

- Is my thesis clear?
- How clear is my thesis?
- How do I know my thesis is clear?
- How can I make my thesis more clear?

You can continue with each element in the description until you have a set of reflection questions for students to use. Or if your students get the hang of this quickly, you can use a few rounds of question generating to demonstrate how to turn descriptions into questions about work, and then have students write their own questions as they reflect.

Feedback on student self-reflection

Asking effective questions about their own work is the first key to supporting students' effective self-reflection. The second, of course, is answering those questions. As students are learning to self-reflect, give them feedback on how well they answer the questions. Feedback on student self-reflection is generally oral, but it can be written if students use a formal self-reflection format. Feedback on student self-reflection need not be given to all students all the time. Feedback on student self-reflection is not used for grades.

Parker and Breyfogle (2011) describe a process of self-reflection that began with Ms. Parker's students using the Math Problem-Solving Rubric to evaluate three anonymous pieces of student work. Later in the project, the class evaluated anonymous work samples from

SELF-REFLECTION

How can you involve students more in self-reflection in your classroom?

a student's Week 1 and Week 4 work and talked about how the rubric described the change. Then Ms. Parker used small-group time to elicit more details about the students' observations of the work by asking probing questions herself. Finally, she used individual conferences to ask students to apply the rubric to their own work. The follow-up questions she used (for example, "You wrote what you did, but did you say why you did it?") functioned as feedback for the students, feeding them forward into their next steps in observation ("No, I just wrote what I did"), and finally to an action plan (writing why).

Summing up

One of the advantages of rubrics is their usefulness for formative assessment. Chapter 9 explored ways to use rubrics to share learning targets and criteria for success with students. Chapter 10 explored ways to use rubrics to develop student work and to give evidence of learning that students can use for further improvement. When students have written, drafted, practiced, honed, and polished, eventually it is time for a grade to certify the level of achievement or accomplishment the students have reached. Chapter 11 discusses ways to use rubrics in grading.

11

How to Use Rubrics for Grading

SELF-REFLECTION

How have you handled using rubrics in grading?
What questions or issues have arisen for you?
How did you resolve them?

Most of this book has been about how to write or select high-quality rubrics and how to use them formatively with students, as an aid to learning. I include this chapter on grading to complete the picture. Sometimes teachers use rubrics well until they get to grading, and then meaning falls apart because rubric levels are not the same kind of numbers as the test scores and percentages most teachers grew up with. Note that this chapter is not a complete treatise on grading, just a discussion of how using rubrics plays out in the grading process. Readers who would like a more complete treatment of grading should consult Brookhart (2011) or O'Connor (2011).

What is grading?

We commonly use the term *grading* to mean two different things. We say, "I graded that assignment" or "I graded that test," meaning a grade was assigned to an individual assessment. We also use *grading* to refer to the process of summarizing a set of individual grades to arrive at a grade for a report card. Report card grades are usually assigned either to a standard or to a subject area, depending on whether the report cards are standards based or traditional. In this chapter, I talk about using rubrics for grading individual assessments and also about summarizing a set of grades that includes rubrics.

Rubric-based grades and percentages—An important difference

Rubrics typically use short scales, often three to six levels. The meaning of the distance between the levels is not the same as for a test, where one point usually means one tiny increment on a scale, either from a right-wrong question or one point on a multipoint question. Rubrics use ordered categories—descriptions of performance along a continuum of quality—for each criterion. For this reason, turning rubrics into percentages, which many people do out of habit or out of the expectations of gradebook software, changes the meaning. For example, a *3* on a four-point rubric typically means "Proficient." Three out of four, however, is 75 percent, which in most grading scales is a *C* and sometimes even a *D*. Neither of those grades means "Proficient."

The goal for all the grading recommendations in this chapter is to have the final grade end up representing, with as much fidelity as possible, the information about student learning contained in individual grades or in the set of grades being combined for a report card grade. Those who are interested in more of the quantitative reasoning behind these recommendations should consult Nitko and Brookhart (2011).

How to use rubrics to grade individual assessments

Use the same rubrics to grade the assignment that students have been using formatively as part of their understanding of their learning target and for monitoring and improving their work. I hope for most readers this is a foregone conclusion.

If students have used rubrics formatively, as they worked, the main "grade" for their assignment should communicate what level they finally achieved on each criterion. This is the information that should be most meaningful to them because it will include descriptions of their work. One good way to do this is to circle the performance-level description that applies to the final work, for each criterion. You don't need to take the time to write that general description, because it is already printed in the rubrics. With the time you save, you can make a few comments specific to the student's particular work—not a lot, as the most effective time for feedback is before work is graded, not after.

If you need an overall grade for a performance assessment graded with analytic rubrics, you can combine the levels achieved for each criterion. Whether you summarize the performance for each criterion into a total-performance description or not, students should see how they scored on each criterion. Criterion-level results provide more useful information for students than one amalgamated score. However, sometimes you need to summarize an overall grade for one assessment for later use in a final grade. Sometimes you don't, as when each criterion is recorded as a grade under a different standard. For example, one rubric score might be recorded under the standard for science content, one for inquiry skills, and one for communication.

If you do need one overall grade (for example, "Science") and must summarize an assessment with one overall score, use the median or mode, *not* the mean, of the scores for each criterion. Figure 11.1 summarizes how to calculate mean, median, and mode, the three most common ways to combine more than one score into a typical score. The figure summarizes all three, even though the median is recommended, so you can see how all three summarize "typical" performance but do so in different ways.

Figure 11.1   Three Ways to Summarize a Set of Scores: Mean, Median, and Mode

Measure of Central Tendency	Example
	On a six-point analytic rubric with four criteria, a student scores 6, 5, 3, 3.
Mean • The sum of all scores divided by the number of scores • Also known as the arithmetic average	**Mean = 4.25** (6 + 5 + 3 + 3)/4 = 4.25

Median
• The score that has half of the scores above and half below it (even if it's between two scores)
• Also known as the 50th percentile
	Median = 4
	(line scores up in order first)
	6 5 3 3
	     ∧
	     4

Mode • The most frequently occurring score in the set of scores • Sometimes helpful to think of it as the "most popular" score	**Mode = 3** (line scores up in order first) 6 5 (3 3)

Figure 11.1 uses as an example a performance that was scored with a six-point analytic rubric with four criteria, on which one student scored *6, 5, 3,* and *3*, respectively. The example assumes all four criteria were of equal weight, which will not always be the case. To weight a criterion more heavily than others to calculate the mean, multiply the weight times the score. For example, to double the weight of the criterion on which

a student scored *6*, for the mean, use *12* instead of *6*, changing the mean to *5.75*. To weight a criterion more heavily than others to calculate the median, repeat it. That is, use two *6*s in the lineup, changing the median to *5*.

I recommend the median for most summarizing purposes. The median is less prone to being pulled by extreme scores than is the mean, as the examples in Figure 11.1 show. And the median is more stable than the mode, as the examples also show. Suppose one of the *3*s in the example had been a *5*? One change in one criterion, probably not representing a hugely different performance overall, would change the overall score by two points—a lot on a six-point scale. Plus the median is easy to calculate—for most analytical rubrics you can just count in your head. In the next section, when I will recommend using the median for summarizing sets of grades on individual assessments, you can let a spreadsheet do your median calculations.

How to combine individual rubric-based grades for a report card grade

The method you choose for combining grades should depend on two things: what types of grades you need to combine and what meaning you want your report card grade to convey. Ask yourself these questions:

- *What kinds of individual grades am I going to summarize for the report card grade?* Are all your individual grades on scales from rubrics, or are your individual grades a mixture of rubrics and percentages? If all your grades are from rubrics, are they all on the same scale? Or were some four-point rubrics, some six-point, and so on? This makes a difference in how you combine them. It's the familiar "apples and oranges" logic. Before you combine numbers meaningfully, they should be on the same scale.

- *How must I report the students' grades on the report card?* Does your report card use letter grades (for example, *A, B, C, D, F*) or percentages or standards-based performance categories? This distinction makes a difference in how you combine individual grades as well.

- *What is my report card grade supposed to mean?* I'll take it as a given that your report card grade is supposed to reflect achievement (as opposed to effort, attendance, and so on). Is achievement reported by subject or by standard on your report cards? The reason this makes a difference for combining grades is that if achievement is separated by standard, you can privilege the most recent evidence; as the student improves on the standard, the grade will go up, even if it started low, because it represents learning in the same domain. If achievement is reported by subject, then the order of the evidence makes less difference, because different standards are covered in different units. Doing poorly on one standard at the beginning of the report period is not subject to revision because of doing well on a different standard toward the end of the report period.

You can use Figure 11.2 to help you decide on a method to use for summarizing your students' individual grades into their report card grades. You will notice in Figure 11.2 that the methods follow three general steps. Each of these steps is worked out in different ways depending on the answers you gave to the three questions (what kinds of grades, how must you report, and what the reported grade is supposed to mean).

The figure lists each question in turn, and then displays two flow charts that start with the answer to the first question. All the recommended methods accomplish these objectives:

- Identify the set of individual grades you are going to summarize, based on what the report card grade is supposed to mean.
- Make sure the individual grades to be summarized are on the same scale.
- Use a summarizing method that expresses in one grade the "typical" achievement level shown in the set of individual grades.

The following sections discusses each of these points in greater detail.

Identify the set of individual grades you are going to summarize, based on what the report card grade is supposed to mean. Usually report card grades are supposed to reflect achievement of a standard or achievement in a subject. It is important to make sure you have recorded grades organized by standard or subject, respectively. That sounds obvious; in fact, it sounds like something you shouldn't need advice about. However, it's worth mentioning, especially in a book on rubrics.

If you used analytic rubrics for a project and are grading by subject, typically you will summarize the set of analytic rubrics for the project into one overall score, as discussed in the previous section of this chapter. However, if you used analytic rubrics for a project and are grading by standard, you may need to keep one or more of the criteria separate. For example, if students wrote a report on an event in history and its effects, and you graded it with the General Rubric for Written Projects in Figure 4.2, the "Content" and "Reasoning & Evidence" scores might be put together to be indicators of a standard about understanding and analyzing historical events, and the "Clarity" score might be an indicator of a standard about communicating about historical events or a standard about expository writing.

Figure 11.2   Decision Tree for Combining Individual Grades for Report Card Summary Grades

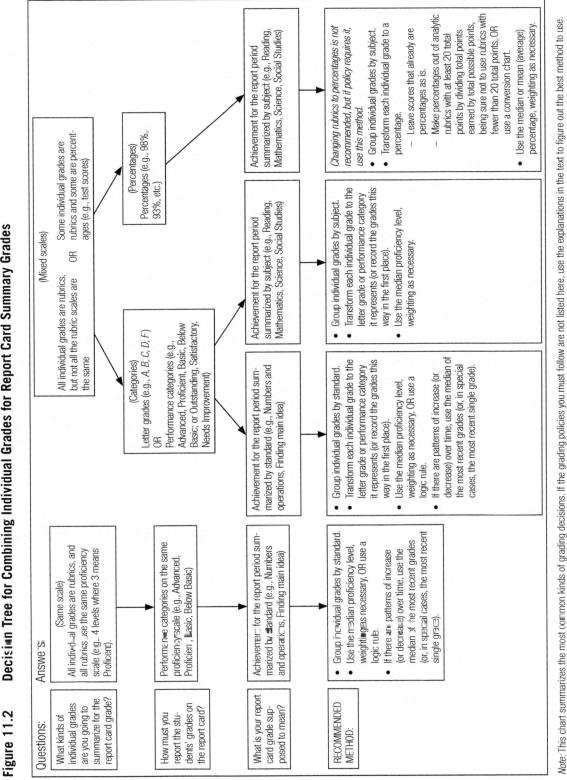

Note: This chart summarizes the most common kinds of grading decisions. If the grading policies you must follow are not listed here, use the explanations in the text to figure out the best method to use.

Therefore, it's very important to know what specific set of information you will need for your report card grade before you record your individual grades. If you have recorded individual grades by standard or subject, as needed, you can easily calculate meaningful report card grades. If you have not, or if you have made overall grades out of rubric results that should have been kept separate, you will not have the right information at hand when it's time to calculate final grades. Even worse, if you recorded improperly organized grades into gradebook software that calculates final grades automatically, you may not even be aware that your final grades do not mean what you intended them to mean.

Begin the report period by selecting the right organization method for your grade records. It's not hard to organize ahead of time. It's very difficult, and sometimes impossible, to reorganize mixed-up results.

Make sure the individual grades to be summarized are on the same scale. Here, the term *scale* means the numbers or levels in which the individual grade is expressed. There might be several different kinds of scales within the set of grades you identified as the set to be summarized for one report card grade. For example, you might have percentages, some four-point rubrics, some six-point rubrics, and so on. Obviously a *4* conveys very different information about achievement on those different scales, and yet if you were to average them, those different meanings would become muddled.

If you have used rubrics with the same proficiency scale for every graded assessment, whether it was a test or performance assessment or project or assignment of any type, your individual grades are already on the same scale for grading purposes. Chapter 6 described how to create this kind of rubric.

If all your recorded grades for individual assignments are from rubrics, but the rubrics have not been designed such that the levels have the same meaning, or if the rubrics do not all have the same number of levels, or both, you need to put them all on the same scale before you combine them. This follows the "comparing apples and oranges" principle. You need to make sure all your rubrics are apples (or oranges, or bananas for that matter); that is, that they are all comparable and can be meaningfully combined.

Whether your set of individual grades is by subject or by standard, if you are reporting in letter grades (for example, A, B, C, D, F) or performance categories (for example, Advanced, Proficient, Nearing Proficiency, Not Yet), or in any other short scale that is really a list of ordered categories of achievement, the easiest thing to do is to transform each individual grade into a category on that scale. Then when you combine the grades, your result will already be on the scale you need, and you'll save yourself having to do a second transformation. I recommend you do this at the time you record each individual grade, but if you haven't, do the transformation before calculating the report card grade.

For example, consider Figure 11.3. The top section lists the grades for five assessments for four students. These grades illustrate a common situation that occurs when teachers have used a mixture of tests or quizzes graded with percentages and performance assessments graded with rubrics. Using multiple, different measures is a good practice. It allows for assessing different aspects of a content domain, at different cognitive levels, and with different performance modalities. It does, however, create a grading situation with incompatible scales, as illustrated in Figure 11.3. Take a moment to verify for yourself that if you simply "averaged" the numbers (added them up and divided by 5), you would get uninterpretable results.

Figure 11.3   Example of Summarizing by Converting Individual Grades to the Scale Used for Reporting

Original Grades for Individual Assessments						
Student	Assessment #1	Assessment #2	Assessment #3	Assessment #4	Assessment #5	
Aiden	79	2	74	3	4	
Brittney	68	2	69	2	3	
Carlos	93	4	98	5	6	
Daniela	88	3	92	5	5	

Transformed Grades, with Report Card Grade (median)						
Student	Assessment #1	Assessment #2	Assessment #3	Assessment #4	Assessment #5	Report Card Grade
Aiden	C	C	C	C	B	C
Brittney	D	C	D	D	0	D
Carlos	A	A	A	A-	A	A
Daniela	B	B	A	A-	A-	A-

Note: The *original grades* for Assessments #1 and #3 were in percentages. The original grades for Assessment #2 were on four-point rubrics with *3* indicating Proficient. The original grades for Assessments #4 and #5 were on six-point rubrics with *4* and above indicating Proficient. The *transformed grades* were put on a letter-grade scale (A, B, C, D, F) because they were to be summarized into a letter grade for the report card.

The solution to this problem is to discern the meaning of each individual grade in terms of the grading scale you must use for reporting so that you can meaningfully combine the results. In this illustration, the report card requires letter grades. If the report card required reporting proficiency levels (Advanced, Proficient, and so on), the procedure would be the same but instead of converting to letters, you would convert to proficiency levels.

In this example, Assessments #1 and #3 were tests, and their results were in percentages. The percentages were transformed to letter grades using the scale 90–100=*A*, 80–89=*B*, and so on, for ease of illustration. You would, of course, use whatever scale was in place in your district or school to do this transformation.

Assessment #2 was a performance assessment scored with four-point rubrics, where *3* was Proficient. These rubric results were transformed to letter grades by a judgment call, that *3* (Proficient) represented *B*-level work, *4* (Advanced) represented *A*-level work, and *2* (Nearing Proficiency) represented *C*-level work. Assessments #4 and #5 were performance assessments scored with six-point rubrics, similar to the 6+1 Trait Writing rubrics, where *4* and above meant Proficient. In this example, to be consistent with the decision to use a *B* to represent Proficient, the six-point rubric was transformed as follows: *6=A, 5=A-, 4=B, 3=C, 2=D, 1=F*. As for the percentage transformations, you would use the conventions in your school or district to transform the rubric results into letters, which would not have to match the transformations in this example.

If you are using rubrics but your report card grades must be expressed in percentages, that's a stickier wicket. Technically you can't add precision (more distinctions or gradations in the scale) that wasn't there in the first place. So mapping a small number of performance categories from rubrics onto a scale with 101 possible points (0 to 100) is not mathematically an appropriate thing to do. If you have to end up with percentages, however, it won't help you much if I just say don't use percentages with rubrics. You would be technically correct but left with no way to report students' grades.

Therefore, I suggest that if you have to report in percentages you work to change your district's reporting system and in the meantime know that you are compromising for the sake of following required policy. If you have to report final grades in percentages, it's better to use judgments about student learning than mathematics that distorts the meaning about student learning. Whether all your recorded grades for individual assignments are from rubrics or some are from rubrics and others are expressed in percentages, you need to put them all on the percentage scale before you combine them.

The purpose is to make sure that they are all comparable and can be combined to yield a meaningful result on the percentage scale.

If you know you need percentages, you can get such scores from rubrics in one of two ways. You can calculate percentages mathematically from your rubrics, or you can use a conversion chart based on judgment.

To calculate percentages from rubrics (I cringe even writing that! What a horrible position to be in!), make sure all the rubrics you use for assignments have at least 20 total points. Thirty is even better. Using at least 20 total points helps address the problem of percentage meanings not coinciding with rubric meanings, which was explained in the introduction to this chapter. (Recall the example that three out of four is 75 percent, which is not "Proficient" on most percentage grading scales).

You won't be able to avoid this problem entirely, but you can improve it a bit by using larger numbers. Five *3*s, on five 4-point rubrics, still yields 75 percent (15 out of 20 possible points). However, in the three-out-of-four case, the scale jumped from 75 percent to 100 percent; it was impossible to score anything in between. With five 4-point rubrics for a total of 20 points, there are possible scores in between (80 percent for four *3*s and a *4*, 85 percent for three *3*s and two *4*s, and so on). The bottom line is, if you have to convert rubrics to percentages—kicking and screaming at compromising information about student learning—at least do it with total points of 20 or more.

I once had a question from a teacher during a workshop on grading. She asked about rubrics in which the lowest category is a *1*. Often the description of performance in the low category includes things like "Answer was unreadable" or even "No answer was given." She was concerned that students would, in effect, be "getting points" for doing no work. That was an interesting question, but it rests on the assumption that the grades are for doing work. Grades are supposed to be measures of achievement, and they are always on arbitrary scales invented by educators. If a student scores 25 percent because of getting five *1*s on an assignment scored with five 4-point rubrics, the student still fails. In fact, that 25 percent is exactly the same as the chance (guessing) score for a multiple-choice test with four-option questions scored right/wrong and then converted to a percentage.

Using a conversion chart based on judgment to transform rubric scores into percentages is a bit more defensible than calculating percentages from rubric scores because the judgments are about what the scores say about student learning. It is still mathematically impossible to make scores more precise than they were in the first place, but at least the judgments can be thoughtful. Figure 11.4 is an example of a conversion chart constructed by using teacher judgment.

Figure 11.4   A Judgment-Based Conversion Chart for Recording Rubric Results as Percentages

Median of Scores for All Criteria on One Assessment	Judgment-Based "Percentage" Grade for That Assessment
4.0	99
3.5	92
3.0	85
2.5	79
2.0	75
1.5	67
1.0	59

The chart in Figure 11.4 reflects judgments about learning. The reasoning flowed from the premise that the *3* was supposed to reflect proficiency and should therefore end up being a "middle *B*" on the percentage scale used in the school. In this example, for ease of illustration we are representing percentages on a scale where 90 to 100 is an *A*, 80 to 89 is a *B*, and so on. Thus, in this conversion chart, a student with performance at the bottom level of the rubric fails but is at the top of the *F* range on the percentage scale. A conversion chart in a school with a different scale would have different numbers. A conversion chart based on different judgments about what the four levels of performance should represent on the scale would also have different numbers.

It is best if conversion charts like this one are constructed by several teachers or a whole department or school. The more perspectives reflected in the judgments, the better. And the more agreement there is about the judgments, the easier it will be to use them and explain them to students and parents.

Finally, to end this section I want to repeat that making percentages out of rubrics is a compromise, and one I'm not happy about. Do it *only* if your grading policies require it.

Use a summarizing method that expresses in one grade the "typical" achievement level shown in the set of individual grades. Once you have your set of individual grades on the same scale—"apples to apples," if you will—you are ready to combine them. For most purposes, I recommend the median. It's an appropriate measure of "typical" performance when the performance measures are ordered categories. Weighting more important grades is easy when you calculate a median (for example, to double, just count the same grade twice; to triple, count it three times). The median does not give any more weight to an extreme low or high score than to any other low or high score.

If you are reporting in letter grades (for example, A, B, C, D, F) *or performance categories (for example, Advanced, Proficient, Nearing Proficiency, Not Yet), or in any other short scale that is really a list of ordered categories of achievement,* use the median letter grade or performance category. You have already transformed each of your individual grades to the reporting scale. Before you take the median, decide if you need to weight any individual grades more than others.

If you are reporting grades by subject, with the individual assignment grades measuring learning on different standards, consider doubling individual grades that reflect more important standards. Or you might consider doubling individual grades that reflect more complex thinking or extended work compared with individual grades that reflect recall and literal comprehension. After you are satisfied that the weights of your individual grades make them contribute their due to the whole set of information, then take the median, as described above and in Figure 11.1. In the example in Figure 11.3, the decision was not to weight any one assessment more heavily than another. Each individual assessment counted the same. The median was used to summarize the set of five grades, and the results are shown in the column labeled "Report Card Grade."

If you are reporting grades by standard instead of subject, with all the assignments representing learning within the same domain, you should still weight individual grades in proportion to the contribution you want them to make to the report card grade. Once you have done that, however, pause before you calculate the median and look for patterns in the individual grades over time. If the pattern looks like a learning curve—that is, it starts low, then rises, and then levels off—those later individual grades in the leveling-off period represent current student achievement of that standard. Take the median of those.

If the pattern is the opposite of that, decreasing over time (rarer, but it happens), you might still take the median of the recent evidence, or you might take the median of all the individual grades to give the student the benefit of the doubt. However, you also need to find out the reason why a student went into a slump. In fact, it's better if you notice the slump before report card time and can do something about it.

If there is no discernible pattern, take the median of all the individual grades. The case of Cort in Figure 6.4 illustrates this scenario.

If you are using rubrics but your report card grades must be expressed in percentages, you have already transformed each of your individual grades into percentages. Give more weight to assessments of more important standards and assessments that measure complex and extended thinking, and less weight to assessments of less important standards and assessments of recall of information. I still recommend

SELF-REFLECTION

Which branches of the decision tree in Figure 11.2 are most relevant to your school and classroom grading policies and needs? How do your grading practices match with the recommendations made in this chapter?

that you use the median percentage as your summary grade. That way you minimize the drastic effect of extreme scores and still report a defensible average grade. (Actually, I recommend the median even for summarizing grades that all began as percentages, not rubrics, for that same reason.) However, you could use the mean percentage as your summary grade as well.

Summing up

This chapter explained how to use rubrics for grading individual assessments and then how to combine them with other individual assessment results for report card grades. In my opinion, the most important aspect of rubrics is how they can be used to describe, develop, and support learning. The grading recommendations in this chapter, for both individual assessments and report cards, are aimed at handling the results of using rubrics for learning in a way that preserves the intended meaning about learning. Because scores from rubrics look like any other numbers, teachers often unknowingly total or average them in ways that are not appropriate for short, ordered-category scales. I hope this chapter has helped you think through the meaning of grades resulting from rubrics.

The chapter recommended report card grading practices based on a series of decisions about grading that depend on the kinds of individual grades you have, the manner in which you must express your report card grade, and the meaning your report card grade is intended to have. That's why there are different recommendations. The chapter, of course, could not cover every possible answer to those three questions. If your situation was not covered, you can still follow the general plan: (1) identify the set of individual grades you need to summarize, (2) put them all on the same scale, and (3) use a summarizing method that is appropriate to the kind of scores you have and that results in the most appropriate message about student achievement.

Afterword

Rubrics are very common but, in my experience, are often poorly handled. It is common to find trivial or list-based criteria (for example, "paragraph has four adjectives"). It is also common to find rubrics used like any other point-based grading scheme, without taking advantage of the formative and student-centered assessment opportunities they afford. And it's very common for grading practices to combine rubrics with test scores and other grades in such a way as to misrepresent student achievement in the final grade. One immediate benefit of this book is that it provides a resource that addresses these common problems.

I believe, however, that this book will be more than an antidote to problems associated with rubrics. With clear explanations and a range of examples, and with the inclusion of instructional strategies to use with rubrics, I hope this book inspires teachers to more effective use of rubric-based assessment and instruction and, in particular, to more involvement of students in their own assessment and learning. Therefore, I hope the book supports teachers and advances student learning. I also

> ### SELF-REFLECTION
>
> What is your current view of rubrics? Compare this reflection with the reflection you made at the beginning of this book.

hope that the examples and explanations support teachers in more active and thoughtful use of rubrics (designing and planning their own rubrics, not just grabbing rubrics from a book or from the Internet). This, too, should lead to more strategic teaching and learning.

Appendix A: Six-Point 6+1 Trait Writing Rubrics, Grades 3–12

6-POINT WRITER'S RUBRIC

IDEAS

	NOT PROFICIENT		
	1 Beginning	**2 Emerging**	**3 Developing**
	No main idea, purpose, or central theme exists; reader must infer this based on sketchy or missing details	Main idea is still missing, though possible topic/theme is emerging	Main idea is present; may be broad or simplistic
A	No topic emerges	Several topics emerge; any might become central theme or main idea	Topic becomes clear, though still too broad, lacking focus; reader must infer message
B	Support for topic is not evident	Support for topic is limited, unclear; length is not adequate for development	Support for topic is incidental or confusing, not focused
C	There are no details	Few details are present; piece simply restates topic and main idea or merely answers a question	Additional details are present but lack specificity; main idea or topic emerges but remains weak
D	Author is not writing from own knowledge/experience; ideas are not author's	Author generalizes about topic without personal knowledge/ experience	Author "tells" based on others' experiences rather than "showing" by own experience
E	No reader's questions have been answered	Reader has many questions due to lack of specifics; it is hard to "fill in the blanks"	Reader begins to recognize focus with specifics, though questions remain
F	Author doesn't help reader make any connections	Author does not yet connect topic with reader in any way, although attempts are made	Author provides glimmers into topic; casual connections are made by reader
Key question: Does the writer stay focused and share original and fresh information or perspective on the topic?			

6-POINT WRITER'S RUBRIC: IDEAS (*continued*)

IDEAS

	PROFICIENT		
	4 Capable	**5 Experienced**	**6 Exceptional**
	Topic or theme is identified as main idea; development remains basic or general	Main idea is well marked by detail but could benefit from additional information	Main idea is clear, supported, and enriched by relevant anecdotes and details
A	Topic is fairly broad, yet author's direction is clear	Topic is focused yet still needs additional narrowing	Topic is narrow, manageable, and focused
B	Support for topic is starting to work; still does not quite flesh out key issues	Support for topic is clear and relevant except for a moment or two	Support is strong and credible, and uses resources that are relevant and accurate
C	Some details begin to define main idea or topic, yet are limited in number or clarity	Accurate, precise details support one main idea	Details are relevant, telling; quality details go beyond obvious and are not predictable
D	Author uses a few examples to "show" own experience yet still relies on generic experience of others	Author presents new ways of thinking about topic based on personal knowledge/experience	Author writes from own knowledge/experience; ideas are fresh, original, and uniquely the author's
E	Reader generally understands content and has only a few questions	Reader's questions are usually anticipated and answered by author	Reader's questions are all answered
F	Author begins to stay on topic and begins to connect reader through self, text, world, or other resources	Author connects reader to topic with a few anecdotes, text, or other resources	Author helps reader make many connections by sharing significant insights into life
Key question: Does the writer stay focused and share original and fresh information or perspective on the topic?			

Appendix A: Six-Point 6+1 Trait Writing Rubrics, Grades 3–12

6-POINT WRITER'S RUBRIC

ORGANIZATION

	NOT PROFICIENT		
	1 Beginning	**2 Emerging**	**3 Developing**
	Organization can't be identified; writing lacks sense of direction; content is strung together in loose, random fashion	Organization is mostly ineffective; only moments here and there direct reader	Organization is still problematic, though structure begins to emerge; ability to follow text is slowed
A	There is no lead to set up what follows, no conclusion to wrap things up	The lead and/or conclusion are ineffective or do not work	Either lead or conclusion or both may be present but are clichés or leave reader wanting more
B	Transitions between paragraphs are confusing or nonexistent	Weak transitions emerge yet offer little help to get from one paragraph to next and not often enough to eliminate confusion	Some transitions are used, but they repeat or mislead, resulting in weak chunking of paragraphs
C	Sequencing doesn't work	Little useful sequencing is present; it's hard to see how piece fits together as a whole	Sequencing has taken over so completely, it dominates ideas; it is painfully obvious and formulaic
D	Pacing is not evident	Pacing is awkward; it slows to a crawl when reader wants to get on with it, and vice versa	Pacing is dominated by one part of piece and is not controlled in remainder
E	Title (if required) is absent	Title (if required) doesn't match content	Title (if required) hints at weak connection to content; it is unclear
F	Lack of structure makes it almost impossible for reader to understand purpose	Structure fails to fit purpose of writing, leaving reader struggling to discover purpose	Structure begins to clarify purpose
Key question: Does the organizational structure enhance the ideas and make the piece easier to understand?			

6-POINT WRITER'S RUBRIC: ORGANIZATION (*continued*)

ORGANIZATION

	PROFICIENT		
	4 Capable	**5 Experienced**	**6 Exceptional**
	Organization moves reader through text without too much confusion	Organization is smooth; only a few small bumps here and there exist	Organization enhances and showcases central idea; order of information is compelling, moving reader through text
A	A recognizable lead and conclusion are present; lead may not create a strong sense of anticipation; conclusion may not tie up all loose ends	While lead and/or conclusion go beyond obvious, either could go even further	An inviting lead draws reader in; satisfying conclusion leaves reader with sense of closure and resolution.
B	Transitions often work yet are predictable and formulaic; paragraphs are coming together with topic sentence and support	Transitions are logical, though may lack originality; ideas are chunked in proper paragraphs and topic sentences are properly used	Thoughtful transitions clearly show how ideas (paragraphs) connect throughout entire piece, helping to showcase content of each paragraph
C	Sequencing shows some logic, but is not controlled enough to consistently showcase ideas	Sequencing makes sense and moves a bit beyond obvious, helping move reader through piece	Sequencing is logical and effective; moves reader through piece with ease from start to finish
D	Pacing is fairly well controlled; sometimes lunges ahead too quickly or hangs up on details that do not matter	Pacing is controlled; there are still places author needs to highlight or move through more effectively	Pacing is well controlled; author knows when to slow down to elaborate, and when to move on
E	Uninspired title (if required) only restates prompt or topic	Title (if required) settles for minor idea about content rather than capturing deeper theme	Title (if required) is original, reflecting content and capturing central theme
F	Structure sometimes supports purpose, at other times reader wants to rearrange pieces	Structure generally works well for purpose and for reader	Structure flows so smoothly reader hardly thinks about it; choice of structure matches and highlights purpose

Key question: Does the organizational structure enhance the ideas and make the piece easier to understand?

Appendix A: Six-Point 6+1 Trait Writing Rubrics, Grades 3–12

6-POINT WRITER'S RUBRIC

VOICE

	NOT PROFICIENT		
	1 Beginning	**2 Emerging**	**3 Developing**
	Author seems indifferent, uninvolved, or distanced from topic, purpose, and/or audience	Author relies on reader's good faith to hear or feel any voice in phrases such as "I like it" or "It was fun"	Author's voice is hard to recognize, even if reader is trying desperately to "hear" it
A	Author does not interact with reader in any fashion; writing is flat, resulting in a disengaged reader	Author uses only clichés, resulting in continued lack of interaction with reader	Author seems aware of reader yet discards personal insights in favor of safe generalities
B	Author takes no risks, reveals nothing, lulls reader to sleep	Author reveals little yet doesn't risk enough to engage reader	Author surprises reader with random "aha" and minimal risk-taking
C	Tone is not evident	Tone does not support writing	Tone is flat; author does not commit to own writing
D	Commitment to topic is missing; writing is lifeless or mechanical; it may be overly technical, formulaic, or jargonistic	Commitment to topic "might" be present; author does not help reader feel anything	Commitment to topic begins to emerge; reader wonders if author cares about topic
E	Voice inappropriate for purpose/mode	Voice does not support purpose/mode; narrative is only an outline; expository or persuasive writing lacks conviction or authority to set it apart from a mere list of facts	Voice is starting to support purpose/mode though remains weak in many places
	Key question: Would you keep reading this piece if it were longer?		

6-POINT WRITER'S RUBRIC: VOICE (*continued*)

VOICE

	4 Capable	5 Experienced	6 Exceptional
	PROFICIENT		
	Author seems sincere, yet not fully engaged or involved; result is pleasant or even personable, though topic and purpose are still not compelling	Author attempts to address topic, purpose, and audience in sincere and engaging way; piece still skips a beat here and there	Author speaks directly to reader in individual, compelling, and engaging way that delivers purpose and topic; although passionate, author is respectful of audience and purpose
A	Author attempts to reach audience and has some moments of successful interaction	Author communicates with reader in earnest, pleasing, authentic manner	Author interacts with and engages reader in ways that are personally revealing
B	Author surprises, delights, or moves reader in more than one or two places	Author's moments of insight and risk-taking enliven piece	Author interacts with and engages reader in ways that are personally revealing
C	Tone begins to support and enrich writing	Tone leans in right direction most of the time	Tone gives flavor and texture to message and is appropriate
D	Commitment to topic is present; author's own point of view may emerge in a place or two but is obscured behind vague generalities	Commitment to topic is clear and focused; author's enthusiasm starts to catch on	Commitment to topic is strong; author's passion about topic is clear, compelling, and energizing; reader wants to know more
E	Voice lacks spark for purpose/mode; narrative is sincere, if not passionate; expository or persuasive writing lacks consistent engagement with topic to build credibility	Voice supports author's purpose/mode; narrative entertains, engages reader; expository or persuasive writing reveals why author chose ideas	Voice is appropriate for purpose/mode; voice is engaging, passionate, and enthusiastic
	Key question: Would you keep reading this piece if it were longer?		

Appendix A: Six-Point 6+1 Trait Writing Rubrics, Grades 3–12

6-POINT WRITER'S RUBRIC

WORD CHOICE

	NOT PROFICIENT		
	1 Beginning	**2 Emerging**	**3 Developing**
	Vocabulary is limited; author searches for words to convey meaning; no mental imagery exists	Vocabulary is flawed, resulting in impaired meaning; wrong words are used; and reader can't picture message or content	Vocabulary is understandable yet lacks energy; some interpretation is needed to understand parts of piece
A	Words are overly broad and/or so generic no message is evident	Words are so vague and mundane that message is limited and unclear	Words are adequate and correct in a general sense; message starts to emerge
B	Vocabulary confuses reader and is contradictory; words create no mental imagery, no lingering memory	Vocabulary has no variety or spice; even simple words are used incorrectly; no mental images exist	Vocabulary is very basic; simple words rule; variety starts to "show" rather than "tell"; mental images are still missing
C	Words are incorrectly used, making message secondary to word misfires	Words are either so plain as to put reader to sleep or so over the top they make no sense	Original, natural word choices start to emerge so piece sounds authentic
D	Misuse of parts of speech litters piece, confusing reader; no message emerges	Redundant parts of speech and/or jargon or clichés distract from message	Rote parts of speech reflect a lack of craftsmanship; passive verbs, overused nouns, and lack of modifiers and variety create fuzzy message
Key question: Do the words and phrases create vivid pictures and linger in your mind?			

6-POINT WRITER'S RUBRIC: WORD CHOICE (*continued*)

WORD CHOICE

	PROFICIENT		
	4 Capable	**5 Experienced**	**6 Exceptional**
	Vocabulary is functional yet still lacks energy; author's meaning is easy to understand in general	Vocabulary is more precise and appropriate; mental imagery emerges	Vocabulary is powerful and engaging, creating mental imagery; words convey intended message in precise, interesting, and natural way
A	Words work and begin to shape unique, individual piece; message is easy to identify	In most cases words are "just right" and clearly communicate message	Words are precise and accurate; author's message is easy to understand
B	Vocabulary includes familiar words and phrases that communicate, yet rarely capture reader's imagination; perhaps a moment of two of sparkle or imagery emerges	Vocabulary is strong; it's easy to "see" what author says because of figurative language—similes, metaphors, and poetic devices; mental imagery lingers	Vocabulary is striking, powerful, and engaging; it catches reader's eye and lingers in mind; recall of handful of phrases or mental images is easy and automatic
C	Attempts at colorful word choice show willingness to stretch and grow, yet sometimes go too far	New words and phrases are usually correct	Word choice is natural yet original and never overdone; both words and phrases are unique and effective
D	Accurate and occasionally refined parts of speech are functional and start to shape message	Correct and varied parts of speech are chosen carefully to communicate message, and clarify and enrich writing	Parts of speech are crafted to best convey message; lively verbs energize, precise nouns/modifiers add depth, color, and specificity
	Key question: Do the words and phrases create vivid pictures and linger in your mind?		

Appendix A: Six-Point 6+1 Trait Writing Rubrics, Grades 3–12

6-POINT WRITER'S RUBRIC

SENTENCE FLUENCY

	NOT PROFICIENT		
	1 Beginning	**2 Emerging**	**3 Developing**
	Sentences are incorrectly structured; reader has to practice to give paper a fair interpretive reading; it's nearly impossible to read aloud	Sentences vary little; even easy sentence structures cause reader to stop and decide what is being said and how; it's challenging to read aloud	Sentences are technically correct but not varied, creating sing-song pattern or lulling reader to sleep; it sounds mechanical when read aloud
A	Sentence structure is choppy, incomplete, run-on, rambling, or awkward	Sentence structure works but has phrasing that sounds unnatural	Sentence structure is usually correct, yet sentences do not flow
B	No sentence sense—type, beginning, connective, rhythm—is evident; determining where sentences begin and end is nearly impossible	There is little evidence of sentence sense; to make sentences flow correctly, most have to be totally reconstructed	Sentence sense starts to emerge; reader can read through problems and see where sentences begin and end; sentences vary little
C	Incomplete sentences make it hard to judge quality of beginnings or identify type of sentence	Many sentences begin in same way and are simple (subject-verb-object) and monotonous	Simple and compound sentences and varied beginnings help strengthen piece
D	Weak or no connectives create massive jumble of language; disconnected sentences leave piece chaotic	"Blah' connectives (and, so, but, then, and because) lead reader nowhere	Few simple connectives lead reader from sentence to sentence, though piece remains weak
E	Rhythm is chaotic, not fluid; piece cannot be read aloud without author's help, even with practice	Rhythm is random and may still be chaotic; writing does not invite expressive oral reading	Rhythm emerges; reader can read aloud after a few tries
Key question: Can you feel the words and phrases flow together as you read it aloud?			

6-POINT WRITER'S RUBRIC: SENTENCE FLUENCY (*continued*)

SENTENCE FLUENCY

	PROFICIENT		
	4 Capable	**5 Experienced**	**6 Exceptional**
	Sentences are varied and hum along, tending to be pleasant or businesslike though may still be more mechanical than musical or fluid; it's easy to read aloud	Some sentences are rhythmic and flowing; a variety of sentence types are structured correctly; it flows well when read aloud	Sentences have flow, rhythm, and cadence; are well built within strong, varied structure that invites expressive oral reading
A	Sentence structure is correct and begins to flow but is not artfully crafted or musical	Sentence structure flows well and moves reader fluidly through piece	Sentence structure is strong, underscoring and enhancing meaning while engaging and moving reader from beginning to end in fluid fashion
B	Sentence sense is moderate; sentences are constructed correctly with some variety, hang together, and are sound	Sentence sense is strong; correct construction and variety are used; few examples of dialogue or fragments are used	Sentence sense is strong and contributes to meaning; dialogue, if present, sounds natural; fragments, if used, add style; sentences are nicely balanced in type, beginnings, connectives, and rhythm
C	Sentence beginnings vary yet are routine, generic; types include simple, compound, and perhaps even complex	Sentence beginnings are varied and unique; four sentence types (simple, compound, complex, and compound-complex) create balance and variety	Varied sentence beginnings add interest and energy; four sentence types are balanced
D	Connectives are original and hold piece together but are not always refined	Thoughtful and varied connectives move reader easily through piece	Creative and appropriate connectives show how each sentence relates to previous one and pulls piece together
E	Rhythm is inconsistent; some sentences invite oral reading, others remain stiff, awkward, or choppy	Rhythm works; reader can read aloud quite easily	Rhythm flows; writing has cadence; first reading aloud is expressive, pleasurable, and fun
Key question: Can you feel the words and phrases flow together as you read it aloud?			

Appendix A: Six-Point 6+1 Trait Writing Rubrics, Grades 3–12

6-POINT WRITER'S RUBRIC

CONVENTIONS

	NOT PROFICIENT		
	1 Beginning	**2 Emerging**	**3 Developing**
	Errors in conventions are the norm and repeatedly distract reader, making text unreadable	Many errors of various types of conventions are scattered throughout text	Author continues to stumble in conventions even on simple tasks and almost always on anything trickier
A	Spelling errors are frequent, even on common words	Spelling is phonetic with many errors	Spelling on simple words is incorrect, although reader can understand
B	Punctuation is often missing or incorrect	Simple end (. ? !) punctuation is correct, internal (, ' ; — : . . .) punctuation is usually wrong or missing	Punctuation is inconsistent
C	Capitalization is random, inconsistent, and sometimes nonexistent	Only the easiest capitalization rules are correctly applied	Capitalization is applied inconsistently except for proper nouns and sentence beginnings
D	Errors in grammar/usage are frequent and noticeable, making writing incomprehensible	Serious grammar/usage problems of every kind make comprehension difficult	Inappropriate grammar/usage results from heavy reliance on conversational oral language; meaning is confusing
E	Extensive editing (on virtually every line) is required to polish text for publication; reader must read once to decode, then again for meaning	There is still a lot of editing required for publication; meaning is uncertain	Too much editing is still needed to publish, although piece begins to communicate meaning

Key question: How much editing would have to be done to be ready to share with an outside source? (Note: For the trait of conventions, grade level matters. Expectations should be based on grade level and include only skills that have been taught. **Expectations for secondary students are obviously much higher than those of the elementary grade levels.**)

6-POINT WRITER'S RUBRIC: CONVENTIONS (*continued*)

CONVENTIONS

	PROFICIENT		
	4 Capable	**5 Experienced**	**6 Exceptional**
	Author has reasonable control over standard conventions for grade level; conventions are sometimes handled well; at other times, errors distract and impair readability	Author stretches, trying more complex tasks in conventions; several mistakes still exist; for secondary students, all basic conventions have been mastered	Author uses standard writing conventions effectively to enhance readability; errors are few and only minor editing is needed to publish
A	Spelling is usually correct or reasonable phonetic on common grade-level words, but not on more difficult words	Spelling on common grade-level words is correct but sometimes incorrect on more difficult words	Spelling is usually correct, even on more difficult words
B	End punctuation is usually correct; internal punctuation is sometimes correct; for secondary students all punctuation is usually correct	Punctuation is correct and enhances readability in all but a few places	Punctuation is correct, creative, and guides reader through entire piece
C	Capitalization is mostly correct	Capitalization is correct; more sophisticated capitalization is used	Capitalization is thoroughly understood and consistently correct
D	Proper grammar/usage remains inconsistent and inaccurate, though problems are not serious enough to distort meaning	Grammar/usage is usually correct; there are few grammar mistakes yet meaning is clear	Grammar/usage is correct and contributes to clarity and style; meaning is more than clear; piece is engaging and inviting to read
E	Moderate editing (a little of this, a little of that) is required to publish; meaning is clear	Several things still need editing before publishing; conventions are more correct than not; meaning is easily communicated	Hardly any editing is needed to publish; author may successfully manipulate conventions for stylistic effect; meaning is crystal clear

Key question: How much editing would have to be done to be ready to share with an outside source? (Note: For the trait of conventions, grade level matters. Expectations should be based on grade level and include only skills that have been taught. **Expectations for secondary students are obviously much higher than those of the elementary grade levels.**)

Appendix A: Six-Point 6+1 Trait Writing Rubrics, Grades 3–12

6-POINT WRITER'S RUBRIC

PRESENTATION

	NOT PROFICIENT		
	1 Beginning	**2 Emerging**	**3 Developing**
	Presentation/formatting of piece confuses message	Presentation/formatting delivers a message clear in places and confusing in others	Presentation/formatting of piece delivers clear message, yet lacks a finished, polished appearance
A	Handwritten letters are irregular, formed inconsistently or incorrectly; spacing is unbalanced or absent; reader can't identify letters	Handwritten letters and words are readable with limited problems in letter shape and form; spacing is inconsistent	Handwriting creates little or no stumbling in readability; spacing is consistent
B	Many fonts/sizes make piece nearly unreadable	Few fonts/sizes make piece hard to read or understand	Fonts/sizes are limited in number; piece starts to come together visually
C	No thought is given to white space—it is random and confusing; identifying beginning and ending of text is difficult	Understanding of white space begins to emerge, though piece seems "plopped" on paper without margins or boundaries	White space begins to frame and balance piece; margins may be present, though some text may crown edges; usage is inconsistent; paragraphs begin to emerge
D	Visuals/graphics/charts are non-existent, incomprehensible, and/or unrelated to text	Visuals/graphics/charts "might" be related to text	Visuals/graphics/charts match and integrate with text at times
E	No markers (title, bullets, page numbers, subheads, etc.) are present	Perhaps one marker (a title, and single bullet or page number) is used	Markers are used but do not organize or clarify piece
Key question: Is the finished piece easy to read, polished in presentation, and pleasing to the eye?			

6-POINT WRITER'S RUBRIC: PRESENTATION (*continued*)

PRESENTATION

	PROFICIENT		
	4 Capable	**5 Experienced**	**6 Exceptional**
	Presentation/formatting of piece works in standard, predictable fashion, delivering a clear message that appears to be finished	Presentation/formatting enhances understanding of message; piece appears finished and is pleasing to eye	Presentation/formatting exceeds best of finished pieces; formatting extends understanding of message; finished appearance is of superior quality
A	Handwriting is correct and readable; spacing is consistent and neat	Handwriting is neat, readable, consistent; spacing is uniform between letters and words; text is easy to read	Handwriting borders on calligraphy; is easy to read and uniformly spaced; pride of author is clear
B	Fonts/sizes are consistent and appropriate; piece is easy to understand	Fonts/sizes invite reader into text; understanding is a breeze	Fonts/sizes enhance readability and enrich overall appearance; understanding is crystal clear
C	White space frames text by creating margins; usage is still inconsistent on the whole; some paragraphs are indented, some are blocked	White space helps reader focus on text; margins frame piece, other white space frames markers and graphics; usage is consistent and purposeful; most paragraphs are either indented or blocked	White space is used to optimally frame and balance text with markers and graphics; all paragraphs are either indented or blocked
D	Visuals/graphics/charts support and consistently clarify text	Visuals/graphics/charts enrich meaning of text and add layer of understanding	Visuals/graphics/charts help enrich and extend meaning by focusing reader's attention upon message
E	Markers are used to organize, clarify, and present whole piece	Markers serve to integrate graphics and articulate meaning of piece	Markers help reader comprehend message and extend or enrich piece
Key question: Is the finished piece easy to read, polished in presentation, and pleasing to the eye?			

Source: Copyright 2010 by Education Northwest. Available at educationnorthwest.org. Reprinted with permission.

Appendix B: Illustrated Six-Point 6+1 Trait Writing Rubrics, Grades K–2

K–2 ILLUSTRATED BEGINNING WRITER'S RUBRIC

IDEAS

Exceptional 6	• The Big Idea is clear and original; the topic is narrowed • Supporting details are relevant, accurate, and specific • Pictures, graphs, charts (if present) clarify the text • Focus: The writing stays on topic • Development is generous and complete
Experienced 5	• The Big Idea is clear; the topic is narrowed • Supporting details are relevant, logical, and mostly accurate • Pictures, graphs, charts (if present) clarify the text • Focus: Usually stays on topic • Development is complete
Capable 4	• The Big Idea is clear, but general—a simple story or explanation • Support is presented in the text • Pictures (if present) support the text • Focus: Generally on topic, with a few missteps • Development is adequate
Developing 3	• The Big Idea is stated in text • Support is minimal • Pictures (if present) offer supporting details • Focus: Limited to one sentence (or repeats the same idea) • Development is simplistic
Emerging 2	• Ideas are conveyed in a general way through text, labels, symbols • Support: Not present in the text • Pictures: Connect with a word, label, symbol • Focus: Unclear or extremely limited • Development: Not present
Beginning 1	• Ideas are unclear; print sense is just beginning • Support: Not present • Pictures: Not clear • Focus: Not present • Development: Not present

K–2 ILLUSTRATED BEGINNING WRITER'S RUBRIC: IDEAS (*continued*)

IDEAS

Exceptional 6	
Experienced 5	
Capable 4	
Developing 3	
Emerging 2	
Beginning 1	

Appendix B: Illustrated Six-Point 6+1 Trait Writing Rubrics Grades, K–2

K–2 ILLUSTRATED BEGINNING WRITER'S RUBRIC

ORGANIZATION

Exceptional 6	• The structure showcases the main idea • Pictures (if present) enhance the text • Transitions are smooth and varied • Sequencing shows planning for impact • An inviting lead and a developed ending are present • Format assists reader orientation
Experienced 5	• The structure is easy to follow • Pictures (if present) clarify the text • Transitions are somewhat varied • Sequencing is sound • An inviting lead and a concluding sentence are present • Format is clear
Capable 4	• Structure is clearly present and complete in a predictable manner • Pictures (if present) show thoughtful placement of elements • Transitions work in a predictable fashion • Sequencing may take a circuitous route, but reader can follow • A beginning, middle, and end are present ("The end") • Format is generally accurate in placement of elements
Developing 3	• A structure is present • Picture elements are placed logically • Transitions are missing or rely upon connectives ("and," "and then") • Sequencing: Not present or confusing • A bare beginning and middle are present—no end • Text and pictures are generally formatted correctly on page
Emerging 2	• Structure is starting to emerge • Pictures show attempt to order/balance elements • Transitions: Not present • Sequencing: Not present • A beginning is attempted—no middle or end • Formatting signs emerging (left-right orientation, picture and text placement, spacing)
Beginning 1	• Structure is not present • Picture elements are random, scattered, or unbalanced • Sequencing and transitions not present • Beginning or ending not present • Format clues: not present

K–2 ILLUSTRATED BEGINNING WRITER'S RUBRIC: ORGANIZATION (*continued*)

ORGANIZATION

Exceptional 6	I went to Yellow stone National Park. It was so cool. When I went I saw Buffalow and one Grizzly Bear. It was funny when we saw the Grizzly Bear cause he was siting down asleep. I like Yellow stone national Park. Do you want to know why I like Yellow stone national Park? Caus you can learn about wild life and the woods.
Experienced 5	Soft Chinchlas my favret anmle is a gray chinchila becuar thay are very very soft and thay are littl I like them becuas Thay are soft thay have big ers so when scary aromls arad Thay no to go the uther way chinchiles lev in the mautens
Capable 4	I like dogs I like dogs thay are soft. Thay are cut they are cool But thay never if me. I jet love dogs. They are Fun. When Ka ke Anna. Me Was Playing Out side Of the Swios Ke Aona Me Wen t high Kia Wen t Slow Ke Anna me Stop Kia then kia Wen t high. The End
Developing 3	
Emerging 2	
Beginning 1	

Appendix B: Illustrated Six-Point 6+1 Trait Writing Rubrics Grades, K–2

K–2 ILLUSTRATED BEGINNING WRITER'S RUBRIC

VOICE

Exceptional 6	• Exceptional expression of feeling, commitment to topic • Pictures (if present) enhance the mood, atmosphere, point of view • Exceptional audience awareness is present; compelling to read • Unmistakably individual; sincere—unique expression
Experienced 5	• The writer's feelings about the subject are loud and clear • Pictures (if present) enrich the mood, atmosphere • Engages the audience ("Did you know?") • Individual and sincere expression
Capable 4	• Identifiable feeling(s) are present in the writing • Pictures (if present) capture the atmosphere or mood in a general way • Audience awareness is present • The individual emerges from the text
Developing 3	• Feeling is expressed in a few words/punctuation ("fun," "like," "favorite," underline, exclamation point) • Pictures show expression in faces and detail • Audience awareness is present in a general way • Individual expression is present
Emerging 2	• A general feeling is captured in words and/or pictures • Pictures capture a mood, simple emotion, or action • Audience awareness: Not yet present or clear • Individual expression is emerging
Beginning 1	• Not enough text is present to convey a mood or feeling • Pictures are hard to interpret • Audience awareness is not yet present • Individual expression is not present

K–2 ILLUSTRATED BEGINNING WRITER'S RUBRIC: VOICE (continued)

VOICE

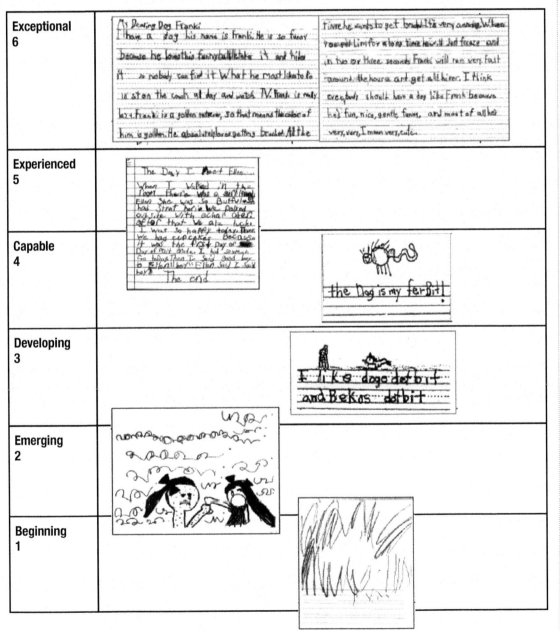

Appendix B: Illustrated Six-Point 6+1 Trait Writing Rubrics Grades, K–2

K–2 ILLUSTRATED BEGINNING WRITER'S RUBRIC

WORD CHOICE

Exceptional 6	• The text is comprised of words that convey a complete message • Word choice includes striking, memorable phrases • Vocabulary reflects precision and accuracy • Repetition is rarely present
Experienced 5	• The text alone conveys the message in several words • Word choice contains moments of sparkle; everyday words used as well • The vocabulary is expanding • Repetition occurs infrequently
Capable 4	• The words stand on their own to convey a simple message • Words are basic and used correctly • Vocabulary is mostly routine, with a few exceptions • Some repetition is present
Developing 3	• Word groups, phrases convey the topic with some help from pictures • Word choice makes sense • Vocabulary is limited to "known" or "safe" words • Repetition of "safe" words and phrases
Emerging 2	• A few words begin to emerge • Word choice is difficult to decode • Vocabulary relies upon environmental print • Repetition: May repeat letters, alphabet, name, etc.
Beginning 1	• No words are present (imitative writing) • Word choice: Not present • Vocabulary: Not present • Repetition: Inconsistent letter shapes, imitative writing or none

K–2 ILLUSTRATED BEGINNING WRITER'S RUBRIC: WORD CHOICE (*continued*)

WORD CHOICE

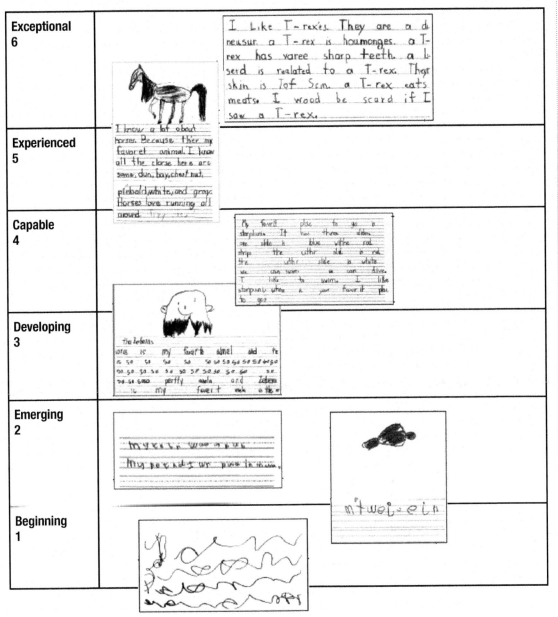

Exceptional 6	
Experienced 5	
Capable 4	
Developing 3	
Emerging 2	
Beginning 1	

Appendix B: Illustrated Six-Point 6+1 Trait Writing Rubrics Grades, K–2

K–2 ILLUSTRATED BEGINNING WRITER'S RUBRIC

SENTENCE FLUENCY

Exceptional 6	• Several sentences are present that vary in structure and length • Sentence beginnings are varied • Rhythm is fluid and pleasant to work with • Connective words work smoothly
Experienced 5	• Several sentences are present and employ more than one sentence pattern • Sentence beginnings are varied • Rhythm is more fluid than mechanical—easy to read aloud • Connective words do not interfere with the fluency
Capable 4	• The writing provides a limited sampling of sentence pattern • Sentences do not always begin the same way • Rhythm is more mechanical than fluid • Connective words show some variation
Developing 3	• Most of a sentence is present, decodable in the text ("Like bunne becuz their riree Fas") • Sentences begin the same way ("I like. . .") • Rhythm is choppy and repetitive • Connective transitions serve as links between phrases ("and," "then," etc.)
Emerging 2	• Part of a sentence may be present ("Cus it is clu") • A word or phrase may be repeated across the page to form the text • Rhythm is not present • Connective words may appear in sentence parts
Beginning 1	• No sentences or sentence parts are present in the text • The marks, lines, or scribbles may imitate writing from left to right • Words stand alone • Connectives: Not present

K–2 ILLUSTRATED BEGINNING WRITER'S RUBRIC: SENTENCE FLUENCY (*continued*)

SENTENCE FLUENCY

Exceptional 6	
Experienced 5	
Capable 4	
Developing 3	
Emerging 2	
Beginning 1	

Appendix B: Illustrated Six-Point 6+1 Trait Writing Rubrics Grades, K–2

K–2 ILLUSTRATED BEGINNING WRITER'S RUBRIC

CONVENTIONS

Exceptional 6	• Capitalization: Accurate for sentence beginnings, proper names, titles • Punctuation: End punctuation, commas in series, other varied uses for stylistic effect • Spelling: Grade level words and "hard" words spelled logically, if not accurately • Grammar and usage: Accurate • Paragraphing: Consistent indention for paragraphs
Experiences 5	• Capitalization: Capitals for sentence beginnings, proper names, titles usually correct • Punctuation: End punctuation usually correct—some varied uses present • Spelling: Usually accurate for grade level words • Grammar and usage: Usually accurate • Paragraphing: First line indented
Capable 4	• Capitalization: Capitals for sentence beginnings, names, titles in evidence • Punctuation: End punctuation is present • Spelling: High use grade level words mostly correct; phonetic spelling easy to decode • Grammar and usage: subject/verb agreement, tense, still spotty • Paragraphing: spotty, or not present
Developing 3	• Capitalization: Beginning sentence, names, title still inconsistent • Punctuation: Period or other punctuation is present somewhere • Spelling: Phonetic spelling decodable; accurate spelling of some words • Grammar and usage: A grammatical construction is present, but missing parts • Paragraphing: Not present
Emerging 2	• Capitalization: Random use of upper and lower case letters • Punctuation: None or random • Spelling: Phonetic, some decodable and/or simple words spelled correctly • Grammar and usage: Part of a grammatical construction is present • Paragraphing: Not present
Beginning 1	• Capitalization: Print sense still emerging • Punctuation: None • Spelling: Pre-phonetic or not present • Grammar and usage: Not present • Paragraphing: Not present

K–2 ILLUSTRATED BEGINNING WRITER'S RUBRIC: CONVENTIONS (*continued*)

CONVENTIONS	
Exceptional **6**	friends are Always Stupendous! A friend is someone you play with at recess. You need to have at least one or two things in common. They need to share toys, and if you are at recess and your friend wants to play, it is not nice to say you can't play. A friend is someone who does not cheat on games or is not a poor sport. A poor sport is someone who they lose a game or get out of a game they start winning or calling you names and say, **I'M NOT PLAYING** **WITH YOU ANYMORE!** One of my favorite things is a friend makes you giggle at jokes that they say, but the bad part is it you giggle at school you can get in trouble by the teachers. You don't have to copy your friend, for example if they like choclate chip cookies and you don't. You should not say "me too!" This is what my friends are like. What is your friend like?
Experiences **5**	 A Baby Elaphent I went to 7h Soo I saw a Ellaphet It was gray and I luvs peanut. It is a baby It loves me. It is so cut It makes me thro a phit
Capable **4**	I like to visit Oragin because I like to visit my Meema. I like to get the big fan leavs that she has. I like to go to the park that we can walk to and play games in the house with Meema.
Developing **3**	My favorite plas is my grmas hous. because I play with my kuns and we go out sid to play out sid.
Emerging **2**	MoMMy haps me onon I got sear band she helps me ohen I chrd cant and she sae me wants the macene and I cant she wants t he menothe onen I feel baohte she shets weah me.
Beginning **1**	

References

Andrade, H. L., Du, Y., & Mycek, K. (2010). Rubric-referenced self-assessment and middle school students' writing. *Assessment in Education, 17*(2), 199–214.

Andrade, H. L., Du, Y., & Wang, X. (2008). Putting rubrics to the test: The effect of a model, criteria generation, and rubric-referenced self-assessment on elementary students' writing. *Educational Measurement: Issues and Practice, 27*(2), 3–13.

Arter, J. A., & Chappuis, J. (2006). *Creating and recognizing quality rubrics.* Boston: Pearson.

Arter, J. A., & McTighe, J. (2001). *Scoring rubrics in the classroom.* Thousand Oaks, CA: Corwin Press.

Arter, J. A., Spandel, V., Culham, R., & Pollard, J. (1994). *The impact of teaching students to be self-assessors of writing.* Paper presented at the annual meeting of the American Educational Research Association, San Francisco. ERIC Document Reproduction Service No. ED370975.

Brookhart, S. M. (1993). Assessing student achievement with term papers and written reports. *Educational Measurement: Issues and Practice, 12*(1), 40–47.

Brookhart, S. M. (1999). Teaching about communicating assessment results and grading. *Educational Measurement: Issues and Practice, 18*(1), 5–13.

Brookhart, S. M. (2010). *How to assess higher-order thinking skills in your classroom.* Alexandria, VA: ASCD.

Brookhart, S. M. (2011). *Grading and learning: Practices that support student achievement.* Bloomington, IN: Solution Tree.

California State Department of Education. (1989). *A question of thinking: A first look at students' performance on open-ended questions in mathematics.* Sacramento, CA: Author. ERIC Document No. ED315289.

Chapman, V. G., & Inman, M. D. (2009). A conundrum: Rubrics or creativity/metacognitive development? *Educational HORIZONS, 87*(3), 198–202.

Chappuis, J. (2009). *Seven strategies of assessment for learning.* Boston: Pearson.

Chappuis, J., Stiggins, R., Chappuis, S., & Arter, J. (2012). *Classroom assessment for student learning: Doing it right—using it well* (2nd ed.). Boston: Pearson.

Chappuis, S., & Stiggins, R. J. (2002). Classroom assessment for learning. *Educational Leadership, 60*(1), 40–43.

Coe, M., Hanita, M., Nishioka, V., & Smiley, R. (2011, December). *An investigation of the impact of the 6+1 Trait Writing model on grade 5 student writing achievement: Final report.* NCEE Report 2012-4010. Washington, DC: U.S. Department of Education.

Goldberg, G. L., & Roswell, B. S. (1999–2000). From perception to practice: The impact of teachers' scoring experience on performance-based instruction and classroom assessment. *Educational Assessment, 6*(4), 257–290.

Hafner, J. C., & Hafner, P. M. (2003). Quantitative analysis of the rubric as an assessment tool: An empirical study of student peer-group rating. *International Journal of Science Education, 25*(12), 1509–1528.

Heritage, M. (2010). *Formative assessment: Making it happen in the classroom.* Thousand Oaks, CA: SAGE.

Higgins, K. M., Harris, N. A., & Kuehn, L. L. (1994). Placing assessment into the hands of young children: A study of student-generated criteria and self-assessment. *Educational Assessment, 2*(4), 309–324.

Kozlow, M., & Bellamy, P. (2004). *Experimental study on the impact of the 6+1 Trait® Writing Model on student achievement in writing.* Portland, OR: Northwest Regional Educational Laboratory. Retrieved January 16, 2012, from http://educationnorthwest.org/webfm_send/134

Lane, S., Liu, M., Ankenmann, R. D., & Stone, C. A. (1996). Generalizability and validity of a mathematics performance assessment. *Journal of Educational Measurement, 33*(1), 71–92.

Moss, C. M., & Brookhart, S. M. (2009). *Advancing formative assessment in every classroom: A guide for instructional leaders.* Alexandria, VA: ASCD.

Moss, C. M., & Brookhart, S. M. (2012). *Learning targets: Helping students aim for understanding in today's lesson.* Alexandria, VA: ASCD.

National Council of Teachers of Mathematics (NCTM). (1989). *Curriculum and evaluation standards for school mathematics.* Reston, VA: Author.

Nitko, A. J., & Brookhart, S. M. (2011). *Educational assessment of students* (6th ed.). Boston: Pearson.

O'Connor, K. (2011). *A repair kit for grading: 15 fixes for broken grades* (2nd ed.). Boston: Pearson.

Parker, R., & Breyfogle, M. L. (2011). Learning to write about mathematics. *Teaching Children Mathematics, 18*(2), 90–99.

Perkins, D. N. (1981). *The mind's best work.* Cambridge, MA: Harvard University Press.

Ross, J. A., Hogaboam-Gray, A., & Rolheiser, C. (2002). Student self-evaluation in grade 5–6 mathematics: Effects on problem-solving achievement. *Educational Assessment, 8,* 43–58.

Ross, J. A., & Starling, M. (2008). Self-assessment in a technology-supported environment: The case of grade 9 geography. *Assessment in Education, 15*(2), 183–199.

Sadler, D. R. (1989). Formative assessment and the design of instructional systems. *Instructional Science, 18,* 119–144.

Wiliam, D. (2011). *Embedded formative assessment.* Bloomington, IN: Solution Tree.

Index

Page numbers followed by *f* denote illustrations.

About the Author

Susan M. Brookhart is an independent educational consultant based in Helena, Montana, and senior research associate at the Center for Advancing the Study of Teaching and Learning in the School of Education at Duquesne University.

She is the author or coauthor of several books and many articles on classroom assessment, including ASCD's *How to Give Effective Feedback to Your Students* and *How to Assess Higher-Order Thinking Skills in Your Classroom*.

Related ASCD Resources: Formative Assessment

At the time of publication, the following ASCD resources were available; for the most up-to-date information about ASCD resources, go to www.ascd.org. ASCD stock numbers are noted in parentheses.

Mixed Media

Formative Assessment Strategies for Every Classroom: An ASCD Action Tool by Susan Brookhart (one three-ring binder) (#707010)

Online Courses

Formative Assessment: The Basics (#PD09OC69)
Formative Assessment: Deepening Understanding (#PD11OC101)

Print Products

Checking for Understanding: Formative Assessment Techniques for Your Classroom by Douglas Fisher and Nancy Frey (#107023)
Classroom Assessment & Grading That Work by Robert J. Marzano
Great Performances: Creating Classroom-Based Assessment Tasks, 2nd ed., by Larry Lewin and Betty Jean Shoemaker
Formative Assessment Strategies for Every Classroom: An ASCD Action Tool, 2nd ed. by Susan M. Brookhart
How to Give Effective Feedback to Your Students by Susan M. Brookhart (#108019)
Transformative Assessment by W. James Popham (#108018)
Learning Targets: Helping Students Aim for Understanding in Today's Lesson by Connie M. Moss and Susan M. Brookhart. (#112002)

Videos and DVDs

The Power of Formative Assessment to Advance Learning (three 30-minute DVDs with a comprehensive user guide) (#608067)

WHOLE CHILD
TENETS

1 **HEALTHY**
Each student enters school healthy and learns about and practices a healthy lifestyle.

2 **SAFE**
Each student learns in an environment that is physically and emotionally safe for students and adults.

3 **ENGAGED**
Each student is actively engaged in learning and is connected to the school and broader community.

The ASCD Whole Child approach is an effort to transition from a focus on narrowly defined academic achievement to one that promotes the long-term development and success of all children. Through this approach, ASCD supports educators, families, community members, and policymakers as they move from a vision about educating the whole child to sustainable, collaborative actions.

4 **SUPPORTED**
Each student has access to personalized learning and is supported by qualified, caring adults.

5 **CHALLENGED**
Each student is challenged academically and prepared for success in college or further study and for employment and participation in a global environment.

For more about the ASCD Whole Child approach, visit **www.ascd.org/wholechild.**

Become an ASCD member today!
Go to www.ascd.org/joinascd
or call toll-free: 800-933-ASCD (2723)